TOWARDS SOCIALISM
OR CAPITALISM?

Leon Trotsky

Towards Socialism
or Capitalism?

NEW PARK PUBLICATIONS

Published by New Park Publications Ltd.,
21b Old Town, Clapham, London SW4 OJT

Towards Socialism or Capitalism? first published in series in *Izvestia* and *Pravda*,
November 1925, as *K sotsializmu ili k kapitalizmu?*

Problems of Development of the USSR first published in *Byulleten Oppozitsii*,
April 1931, as *Problemy razvitiya SSSR.*

Soviet Economy in Danger first published in *Byulleten Oppozitsii*,
November 1932, as *Sovetskoe khozyaistvo v opastnosti!*

Foreword
Copyright © New Park Publications Ltd.,
1976

Set up, Printed and Bound
by Trade Union Labour

Distributed in the United States by:
Labor Publications Inc.,
135 West 14 Street, New York
New York 10011

ISBN 0 902030 85 X

Printed in Great Britain by
Astmoor Litho Ltd. (TU),
21-22 Arkwright Road, Astmoor, Runcorn, Cheshire

Contents

CONTENTS

Foreword

The reader will find in this volume three of Trotsky's major writings on the Soviet economy in the period from 1925 to 1932. This was the period of Stalinist degeneration and Trotsky's fight against it. To extract the full value of these writings for today, they must be seen in this historical context, while it must be emphasized that they have more than an historical interest.

Besides representing important stages in Trotsky's analysis of the Soviet economy in the period before and after the rise of the Stalinist bureaucracy, they are an important contribution to the general theory of socialist economic planning and provide guidelines for the revolutionary party in formulating its economic policy and in carrying it out after the taking of power. The Soviet experience, despite its very specific character, was, and is, nevertheless a great laboratory for establishing the superiority of planning over the anarchic market economy of capitalism and for learning from the gross mistakes and miscalculations perpetrated by the Stalinist bureaucracy. Trotsky sought both to guide and then to criticize the economic policy of the workers' state as well as to draw all the lessons from its experience for the international working class confronted with the task of developing the productive forces far beyond the level attained by crisis-ridden capitalism.

The first successful working class revolution took place in one of the most backward capitalist states, Tsarist Russia, then predominantly an agrarian country with a vast peasantry. The failure of the revolution to spread to the advanced countries of Western Europe, the conditions of civil war and military intervention by the imperialists, confronted the Bolsheviks with immense problems of a quite new and unsuspected character. To cope with the emergency the policy of War Communism was introduced. Inevitable in the circumstances it evoked considerable opposition from the peasantry and operated, in any case, in a country impoverished by years of war and civil war in which industrial production had fallen to less than one-fifth of its pre-war level. It was necessary, therefore, to make a retreat and at the Tenth Congress of the Communist Party in March 1921 the New Economic Policy was adopted. In order to rebuild the economy a measure of private trade was permitted in the hands of the so-called Nepmen, the requisitioning of grain was abolished and a tax in grain and later money substituted as a concession to the peasantry. The 'commanding heights' of industry, finance and transport remained in the hands of the state and its planning organs headed by the State Planning Commission (Gosplan). The period of the NEP was one of intense and, for the first years, uninhibited economic debate in which all the great issues of planning were thoroughly discussed at a high theoretical level. The main division was between those who saw NEP persisting for a lengthy period with all the necessary concessions to the rich peasants (kulaks) and Nepmen, whose main spokesman was Bukharin, and the Left Opposition, standing for the fastest tempos of growth possible and a rapid transition to planned industrialization and the voluntary collectivization of the agrarian sector.

But this was no academic debate because it was intertwined with a major political division between irreconcilable tendencies within the party. Stalin, who as General Secretary, had assumed control over the party apparatus after the death of Lenin, proclaimed the revision of Marxist theory in the form of 'socialism in one country'. One aspect of this was the attack on 'Trotskyism' and Trotsky himself was shunted into economic posts where it was hoped that he would be out of the way. Undeterred, Trotsky continued the struggle, if in a veiled form, in writings such as *Towards Socialism or Capitalism? (Whither Russia?)* This was published in serial form in *Pravda*, the party daily, and translated into many languages including English (it was first published in this country by Methuen in 1926).

In this pamphlet Trotsky draws up a balance sheet of the first eight years of the Soviet economy and principally of NEP. In it he laid emphasis not on the concessions to capitalism in the NEP but on the vital importance of the commanding position occupied by the state and the decisive nature of the competition (or conflict) between them. It was necessary therefore to develop a policy in all spheres which could ensure the victory of socialist planning over the tendencies working towards a restoration of capitalism. He analysed the conditions for this victory and from the figures drew the conclusion that victory was being won.

Despite his justified optimism, however, Trotsky was far from being complacent. On a world scale the decisive test would be the productivity of labour, the rate of growth of output and its qualitative improvement. Here Russia still lagged far behind and there was no point in disguising the fact. Only the monopoly of foreign trade could prevent the swamping of the market by cheap capitalist goods, and even that was not all-powerful. Trotsky therefore sketched out a policy for industrial advance and for making use of the world market to strengthen socialised industry.

Trotsky explicitly says that: 'In the whole of my essay I have confined myself exclusively to the economic process and to its logical development, so to speak. Thus, I have consciously excluded from my field of vision all other factors not only influencing economic development but capable of diverting it in another direction.' He excluded the political conditions, internal and international, no doubt in part because of his disputed position in the party and the danger of being accused of factionalism in a work of this kind. However, he did not refrain from pointing out that in the final analysis the questions facing the Soviet economy would be settled on the arena of the world proletarian revolution — which his enemies, adherents of the 'theory' of socialism in one country, denied.

The second of the articles republished here was written in 1931 after Trotsky had been hounded from the Soviet Union and was living as an exile in Turkey. However, contrary to the expectations of the Stalinist bureaucracy, Trotsky had not gone over to the bourgeoisie or buried himself in historical work. Notwithstanding that it was at this time that he wrote his massive *History of the Russian Revolution*, Trotsky considered his main task to be to build an international opposition, continuing the work of the Left Opposition, for which he had been expelled from Russia, to change the leadership of the Communist Parties and the Soviet Union.

The Theses on 'Problems of the Development of the USSR' were written during the First Five Year Plan when the bureaucracy was making the most extravagant claims. After the 'semi-capitulation' to the kulaks prior to 1928 the Stalinists plunged into forced collectivization in a desperate attempt to solve the grain crisis. They not merely liquidated the kulaks as a class but launched a ferocious war on a large section of the peasantry, physically liquidating millions of people. Soviet agriculture has never recovered. Shortly afterwards, with equal lack of preparation, the Five Year Plan inaugurated a massive programme of industrialization by the same bureaucratic methods. The key to this left zigzag was to be found in the bureaucratic degeneration analysed by Trotsky and the adoption of the theory of 'socialism in one country'.

Trotsky insisted that the conquests of October had not been overthrown and that the Soviet Union remained a workers' state as defined by its property relations. He still believed at this time (1931), that the party could be revived and that regime regenerated through a programme of reforms. It was not until after the defeat of the German proletariat in 1933 at the hands of the Nazis following the imposition of the disastrous policy of 'social fascism' on the German Communist Party that Trotsky concluded that it was necessary to build new parties and a new International and carry out a political revolution against the bureaucracy as a caste of usurpers.

The writings of 1931 thus came before the full extent of the disastrous course of the bureaucracy became visible. To some extent, as with the question of the trials of the Mensheviks, Trotsky took the official propaganda at its face value. Likewise he underestimated the depths of cynicism and brutality to which the bureaucracy would descend even on such matters as the treatment of the peasantry. He could still hope that the Bolshevik-Leninist faction in the Soviet Union would be able to exercise an influence on the course of events, though most of its members would either capitulate (or had already done so) or would be rounded up and sent to the camps or physically wiped out.

While recognizing the achievements of the first years of the Five Year Plan Trotsky rejected the arrogant and false claims of the bureaucracy and warned of the great dangers facing the Soviet economy. His summing up of the first two years, 'The Soviet Economy in Danger' (1932) attracted international attention. Hailing the achievements of the Soviet planned economy, he attacked the 'light-minded adventurism' of the boasts that the Plan would be fulfilled in four years.

In fact, in this article Trotsky laid his finger on fundamental defects of bureaucratic planning of the kind which still dog the Soviet economy. These include the permanent nightmare of disproportions between the different sectors of industry; the tendency to commence

too many capital projects and thus have scarce resources tied down in
work in progress; the poor quality results from hastiness in an attempt
to fulfil targets on time; the enormous sacrifices imposed on the
working class.

Trotsky laid stress on the serious situation created by forced collectivization, the danger of inflation resulting from the paying out of
money incomes in excess of the supply of consumer goods and the
operation of the open market for part of the produce of the collective
farms. He insisted that at the stage reached by the Soviet economy 'the
plan is checked and, to a considerable measure, realized through the
market'. It could not be determined by the will of the bureaucracy, or
rather to the extent that it was it could only mean adventuristic tempos
of growth, massive disproportions and crises resulting from lack of
reserves. The same problems, the same crises of underproduction,
still afflict the Soviet economy today despite all the progress which has
been achieved thanks to the nationalized property relations and the
planned economy.

Needless to say Trotsky's warnings went unheeded. Instead, under
Stalin the bureaucracy pushed the economy blindly forward unleash-
ing an unprecedented reign of terror against the working class, inside
and outside the party. In reading this article today it must be remem-
bered that Trotsky still believed it possible to reverse the Stalinist
course with a policy of reforms. Hence his call for a temporary
retreat, what would now be called a 'plan holiday', between the First
and the Second Five Year Plan to enable the tremendous mistakes to
be rectified and planning to be placed on a new basis. This was to be
Trotsky's last effort to put forward a reform programme for the Soviet
Union. Within months it was to be outpaced by events.

The defeat of the German working class required a re-assessment of
the role of the bureaucracy and the nature of Stalinism. It showed that
it had passed definitively to the camp of counter-revolution and was
now bent upon maintaining the status quo and peaceful coexistence
with capitalism as the necessary corollary of the policy of 'socialism in
one country'. Trotsky remained as before convinced that the conquests of October had not been filched away, that the bureaucracy had
not assumed the attributes of a class but was a parasitic growth on the
workers' state. But he now proclaimed the necessity for the political
revolution and the formation of new revolutionary parties as the only
way to safeguard these conquests and extend them on a world scale.

This required a new analysis of the Soviet Union and an assessment of the Plans on which Trotsky was shortly to embark, finding its mature expression in *The Revolution Betrayed* (1936). The articles in this volume should thus be studied in their historical setting as part of the development of the thought of the leading Marxist of his time and part of the theoretical heritage of the movement. We are confident that we have in the socialist planned economy an alternative to capitalism now more than ever necessary as the world crisis deepens. Trotsky drew from Soviet experience serious lessons which will prove invaluable in carrying out the practical tasks of planning. Above all he held clear the difference between the results of the rule of the bureaucracy which usurped power in the first workers' state and still holds it because of its backwardness and isolation and the failure of the revolution to spread, and the impressive achievements of the planned economy in this same unpromising environment. Once the working class takes power in the advanced countries there can be no doubt that planning will make possible unprecedented material and cultural advances leaving far behind the impressive but still flawed achievements of the first workers' state. That was always the vision in Trotsky's mind as he dealt with the problems of the Soviet economy, in contrast with the bragging self-satisfaction and nationalist self-sufficiency of the advocates of 'socialism in one country'.

Towards Socialism
or Capitalism?

1925

To the English reader

This book is an attempt to estimate the true value of the foundations of our economic development. The difficulty of an evaluation of this kind lies in the sharp break made by our development. When a movement proceeds along a straight line, two points are sufficient to determine its course. On the contrary, should development describe a complex curve the estimation of each separate section becomes a difficult matter. And the eight years of the new regime are merely a small section.

Our opponents, however, and our enemies have repeatedly passed severe judgment on our economic development — and that long before the eighth anniversary of the October Revolution. Their judgments follow two lines: in the first place they tell us that in building up a socialist economy we are ruining the country, in the second they say that in developing our productive forces, we are practically marching towards capitalism. The first method of judgment is characteristic of pure bourgeois thought; the second is as typical of social-democratic i.e. disguised bourgeois ideology. There is no sharp line of demarcation between the two types of criticism and the two often exchange weapons in a neighbourly way — without noticing it themselves — in the intoxication of their battle against communist barbarity.

The present work will show, I hope, to the unbiased reader that the outspoken big bourgeois and the petty bourgeois masquerading as socialists deliberately pervert the truth. They do so when they say that the Bolsheviks have ruined Russia. The most incontestable evidence bears out the fact that in Russia, ruined first by the Imperialist war and then by the civil war, the productive forces of trade and agriculture are approaching the pre-war level which will be attained in the course of the current year. They are also wrong when they say that the development of our productive forces proceeds on capitalist lines. In all branches of the economic life — in industry, transport, trade, the credit system — the predominance of State management, far from diminishing with the growth of the productive forces, is steadily increasing. This is fully borne out by figures and facts.

The problem of agriculture is a much more complicated one, and there is nothing surprising in this to the Marxian mind. The change from the system of small individual peasant holdings to socialist methods of land cultivation is only conceivable after a number of consecutive stages of progress in technical science in economics and culture. The all important condition of the change is that power should remain in the hands of the class whose object is to lead the community towards socialism and which gains more and more ability to influence the peasantry by means of State industry and improved scientific agriculture, creating thereby premises for a transition to collective methods of cultivation.

We have obviously not yet solved this problem. We are only creating the premises for a consecutive and gradual solution of it. These very premises, however, develop new disparities and pitfalls. What are they?

At present the State places on the market four-fifths of the industrial produce, while about one-fifth falls to the share of private enterprise, practically all provided by the petty home industries. Railway and water transport is entirely in the hands of the State. State and co-operative trade now covers nearly three-quarters of the trade turnover. Ninety-five per cent of foreign trade is in the hands of the State. Credit institutions form a centralized State monopoly. This mighty State combine, however, is confronted by no less than 22,000,000 peasant holdings. A combination of State economy and peasant economy subject to a general growth of the productive forces, at present constitutes the fundamental *social* problem of socialist progress in our country.

The growth of the productive forces is an indispensable condition of the achievement of socialism. At the present level of economic development and culture, the growth of the productive forces is made possible only by the inclusion of the individual interest of the producers into the scheme of communal economy. In regard to industrial workers, this is secured by making the wages dependent on output. Much success has already been achieved in this direction. In regard to the peasants, personal interest is secured by the very existence of individual holdings and their participation in the market. But there are also difficulties arising from the same fact. Differences in the scale of wages, however considerable they may be, do not lead to a stratification of the proletariat; the workers, no matter what their wages are, remain workers employed in State factories and works. The case is different in regard to the peasants. With 22 million peasant holdings working for the market, the State farms, collective peasant farms and agricultural communes forming but an insignificant minority among them, we are inevitably led to the position where at the one extreme of the peasant masses we have not only prosperous but exploiting farms; at the other, a part of the less prosperous are falling into pauperism, and paupers becoming hired labourers. When the Soviet Government, on the advice of our Party, introduced the New Economic Policy and widened its scope in regard to the land, it was quite aware of the inevitable social results on the economic system, as well as of the political dangers it involved. However, we regard these dangers not as fatal consequences to be accepted, but as problems which have to be carefully analysed and solved at each successive stage of our development.

The danger might have become insuperable had the State given up its direction of industry, trade and finance at the same time as the stratification among the peasant masses was gaining ground. Had that been the case the influence of private capital would have grown on the market, the peasant market first of all, and in accelerating the process of stratification among the peasantry might have turned the whole of the economic development towards capitalism. That is the reason why it was so very important for us to make sure, first of all, in what direction the change was taking place in relation to the class forces in industry, transport, finance, home and foreign trade. The growing predominance of the socialist State in all these branches — the State Planning Commission proves this beyond a doubt — has created quite a new relation between the town and the land. We stand firmly at the posts of command at the head of economic development, and the growth of capitalist or semi-capitalist tendencies in agriculture cannot possibly at any conceivable time in the near future pass beyond our control. And to gain time in this matter is to gain all. As far as there is struggle between the capitalistic and socialistic tendencies in our economic life — it is the co-operation and competition between them which actually constitute the essence of the New Economic Policy — the issue of the struggle depends on the rate of development of the two tendencies. In other words should State industry develop more *slowly* than agriculture and should the latter *with increasing speed* produce the two opposite poles we have spoken of — the capitalistic farmers at the top, the proletarians at the bottom — this would, of course, lead to a restoration of capitalism. But let our enemies but attempt to prove such an issue to be *inevitable*. They will burn their fingers at the task even if they attack the question more skilfully than poor Kautsky did (or Mr. MacDonald). But is such a possibility *out of the question?* Theoretically it is not. Should the party in power make blunder after blunder in politics and economics and thus impede the growth of industry which is now developing in so promising a way, should it let out of its hands the control of the political and economic processes going on in the rural districts, the cause of socialism in our country would certainly be lost. In our prognosis, however, we have no desire to anticipate such possibilities. How to lose power, how to give up all the conquests of the proletariat, how to help the cause of capitalism has been admirably taught us by Kautsky and his friends after November 9, 1918. There is nothing more to be added to that. Our problems, our aims, our methods are different. We want to show how to keep and to consolidate the power gained by the proletariat, and how to pour socialist economics into the mould of the proletarian State. We have every reason to anticipate that, with proper guidance, the growth of industry will keep ahead of the process of stratification going on among the peasantry and neutralise it, creating a technical base and economic possibilities for a gradual transition to collective farming.

This work does not give statistical details of the stratification going on among the peasantry, for the very reason that such statistics as are needed for a *general* estimation of the process do not exist; not so much because of the deficiencies in our public statistics, as of the peculiar character of a social process embracing the molecular changes of 22 million peasant farms. The State Planning Commission, whose esti-mates form the base of the present work, is now investigating the process of the economic stratification going on among the peasantry.

The conclusions it will arrive at will be published in due course, and will certainly be of the utmost importance for the measures to be adopted by the State in regard to taxation, agricultural credits, co-operation, etc. These statistics, however, will by no means alter anything in the main forecasts of the present work.

Kislovodsk
November 7, 1925
The eighth anniversary of the October Revolution

CHAPTER ONE

The Language of Figures

I

The State Planning Commission has published the control figures of the Soviet national economy for the financial year 1925-1926. This may sound dry and bureaucratic, but in the dry columns of figures and in the equally dry explanations of them, we can hear the glorious music of socialism in growth. Here, we no longer have conjectures, propositions, hopes, theoretic speculations; here we have the weighty tongue of numbers, convincing even to the New York Stock Exchange. We will pause at these figures, at the most important of them, for they are fully worth it.

First of all, the very fact of their publication is a glorious event for us. The day on which they appeared (August 20) should be marked on the Soviet calendar. Agriculture, industry, home and foreign trade, the volume of money in circulation, prices of commodities, credit operations, the State budget, are all shown in these figures in the process of their development and correlation. We have here a clear and comprehensible comparison of all the important figures for 1913, for 1924-1925, and the estimates for the year 1925-1926. The explanatory notes give all the necessary data for the other years of the Soviet economy. As a result, we receive a general picture of our process of construction, as well as an estimate for the succeeding financial year. That this has been possible is an achievement of the first order.

Socialism is a balance sheet. Only, under the New Economic Policy the forms of it are different from those we attempted to adopt under War Communism. The latter can only find full expression under socialism completely realized. But socialism is a matter of a balance

9

sheet even now, and under the New Economic Policy still more than under complete socialism, for then the contents of the balance sheet will be purely economic, whereas now it is bound up with the most complicated political problems. And here, in this table of control figures, the socialist state is for the first time taking stock of all the branches of its economic system in their correlation and development. Its very possibility is a sure sign of concrete economic success, as well as of a growing ability to calculate, to generalize, and to lead in the economy. The control figures may be regarded as a sort of matriculation. We must bear in mind however, that matriculation is not equal to graduation. It is only the passage from secondary to higher education.

When we look at the figures, the first question that arises is, how far are they correct? In this respect, there is a wide field for reserves, restrictions, and even scepticism. We know that our statistics and figures are often inaccurate, not so much because of less efficiency than is to be found in other branches of our economic and cultural activities, but because they reflect all, or at least, many aspects of our backwardness. This, however, does not justify a wholesale disbelief in them in the hope that in a year or two perhaps, one might be able to show up some error in one or other of the figures and pose as being wise after the event. There will most probably be many errors, but wisdom after the event is the very cheapest wisdom of all. For the moment, the figures of the State Planning Commission give the closest approximation to truth. Why? For three reasons. First of all, they are founded on the most complete material available, and material moreover, which has not been obtained from the outside, but has been evolved day in, day out, by the different sections of the Commission itself. Secondly, the material has passed through the hands of the most competent and qualified economists, statisticians, and engineers, and thirdly, the work has been carried out by an institution which is free from all departmental partiality and can always confront the different departments when necessary.* There are moreover, no commercial and no economic secrets generally for the State Planning Commission, for it has the right to verify either directly or through the

---

* The control figures of the active economic organizations are 'not only deficient, they are moreover purposely so,' says a note of the explanatory pages of the State Planning Commission. This hard judgment should be particularly noted. With the help of the State Planning Commission and the press, the active economic organizations must be taught to give disinterested, i.e., correct figures.

Workers' and Peasants' Control Department any productive process or trade account. All balance sheets are open to its inspection, as well as departmental estimates, and not merely from their show-front but from their rough draft. Some of the figures, of course, are bound to be disputed one way or another by the different departments. The objections, whether accepted or refuted, may seriously influence the work to be done for current practical purposes, such as import and export operations or the allocation of revenues for economic needs etc., but such adjustments will not affect the figures in the main. Figures more reliable, or more carefully weighed and examined than the control figures of the State Planning Commission cannot be had at the present time. At any rate, even provisional figures, based on all the preceding work, are infinitely preferable to working in the dark. In the first place, we make our adjustments as a result of experience and thus learn something, in the second, we are living in a haphazard way.

The control figures take us to October 1, 1926. This means that in about twelve months, when we shall be in possession of the actual figures for the financial year, 1925-26, we shall be able to compare our activities of to-morrow with our provisional estimates of today. No matter how widely the two may differ, the comparison of the figures will in itself be invaluable as a lesson in planned economics.

When we speak of the accuracy of the provisional estimates, we must first of all clearly understand of what kind the estimates are. When the statisticians of, let us say, the Howard Institute of America, try to determine the tendencies or the rate of growth of different branches of the American economy, they proceed to some extent like the astronomers — they try to grasp the dynamics of processes completely outside their control, with the difference only that statisticians do not possess anything like the precise methods of astronomers. The position of our statisticians is, in principle, a different one. They are on the staff of organizations which take an active lead in economics. And estimate is not a passive thing, but a lever of positive economic provision. Each figure is not only a photograph, but also an order. The control figures have been prepared by a state institution having the highest command of the economy (and what command!). When the figures say that our exports have to increase from 462,000,000 roubles to 1,200,000,000 roubles in the financial year, 1925-26, that is to say, by 160 per cent, it is not merely a forecast but a definite objective to be obtained. On the basis of what is, the figures show what has to be done. When the figures say that the amount of capital to be put into industry, i.e. the cost of reconstruction and expansion of basic capital is to be 900,000,000 roubles, it is again not a passive estimation, but a practical task of the greatest importance, based on statistics. Such is the table of control figures from beginning to end. It is a dialectical combination of theoretical anticipation with practical insight, the consideration of objective conditions and tendencies together with subjective conceptions of economic problems on the part of the Workers' and Peasants' State. Herein lies the great difference between the control table of the State Planning Commission and the figures and all sorts of estimates of any capitalist state. Herein, as we shall see later, lies the immense superiority of our, that is to say, socialist methods, to those of capitalism.

The control estimates of the State Planning Commission provide, however, not so much a statistical appraisement of socialist economic methods in general, as the adaptation of these methods to the particular needs of the stage we have reached in our New Economic Policy. The elemental processes of economics specially admit of objective statistical treatment. In their turn, the economic processes directed by the State, emerge on the market at one stage or another and market methods bring them in contact with the uncontrolled processes produced by the split-up condition of peasant agriculture. State planning at the present moment largely consists in combining the controlled and directed processes with the uncontrolled elemental processes of the market. In other words, in our economics, socialist tendencies in varying stages of development are combined and interwoven with capitalist tendencies, also in varying stages of maturity and immaturity. The control figures connect certain processes with others and thus establish the equilibrium of development. This is the main importance of a provisional plan for socialism.

That the economic processes developing in our country are of a deeply opposite nature, representing a struggle between two systems mutually excluding each other — between socialism and capitalism — we have always known and never attempted to hide. On the contrary, at the very moment when we passed to the New Economic Policy, Lenin put the gist of the position clearly in his historic question 'Who is going to score?' Menshevik theoreticians, Otto Bauer first among them, condescendingly hailed the New Economic Policy as a sober capitulation of premature, violent Bolshevik methods of socialist economics to the tried and tested road of capitalism. The fears of some and the hopes of others have been seriously tested, and the result is given in the control figures of our social and economic estimates. The great significance of the estimates lies in the fact that speculation on the socialist and capitalist elements of our economy, on plans and conditions generally is no longer possible. We have taken stock of our resources, it may be roughly and provisionally, but we have quantitatively determined the relation between capitalism and socialism in our economy, and have done this for today and tomorrow. Thanks to this, we have obtained valuable, concrete material for a reply to the historic question, 'Who is going to score?'

II

All that has been said so far merely relates to the principle of the control figures of the State Planning Commission. We have shown the enormous importance for us of having at last achieved the possibility of estimating the basic processes of our economy in their correlation and development and of thus having obtained a vantage ground for an infinitely more conscious and provident planning policy, and that not only in the sphere of the economy. But what is of greater importance to us, of course, is the actual content of the control estimates, that is to say, the figures which indicate our social development.

In order to receive a proper answer to the question, 'Are we heading for socialism or capitalism?' we must , first of all, properly formulate the question itself. It naturally divides into three subsidiary questions: (a) Are our productive forces developing? (b) What are the social forms of this development? (c) At what rate does the development proceed?

The first question is the simplest of all and at the same time the most fundamental. Neither capitalism nor socialism are thinkable without the development of productive forces. War Communism which grew out of historic necessity, was soon played out, having stopped the development of the productive forces. The most rudimentary and the most imperative principle of the New Economic Policy was to develop the productive forces as a basis for social development in general. The New Economic Policy was greeted by the bourgeoisie and the Mensheviks as an indispensable, but, of course, 'inadequate' step towards the liberation of the productive forces. Menshevik theoreticians of the Kautsky and Otto Bauer type approved the New Economic Policy. They regarded it as the dawn of a capitalist restoration in Russia. They added that the New Economic Policy would either break the Bolshevik dictatorship (a happy issue), or the Bolshevik dictatorship would break the New Economic Policy (an unhappy issue). Converts to Bolshevism from the opponents' ranks were at the outset chiefly attracted by the supposition that the New Economic Policy would ensure the development of the productive forces along capitalist lines. It is here that the control figures of the State Planning Commission provide fundamental elements for an answer to the question, not only regarding the development of the productive forces in general, but as to the lines this development is taking.

We are well aware, of course, that the social form of our economic development is dual, being founded both on collaboration and on the struggle between capitalist and socialist methods, forms and aims. Such are the conditions our development has been placed in by the New Economic Policy. In fact, they form the very essence of the New Economic Policy. We can, however, no longer be satisfied by such a general conception of the contradictory forces of our development. We need and demand the most accurate coefficients for our economic contradictions, not only the dynamic coefficients of our general development, but the relative coefficients of the weight of the one or other tendency. On the answer to this question a great deal, even everything, depends, in our home as well as our foreign policy.

To put it at its sharpest we will say that without an answer to the question concerning the relative strength of capitalist and socialist tendencies and the direction in which the relative strength of each is modified in accordance with the growth of the productive forces, we cannot arrive at a clear and precise estimation of the chances and possible dangers of our peasant policy. As a matter of fact, if it should happen that in the development of our productive forces capitalist tendencies were growing at the expense of socialist tendencies, the final expansion of individualistic tendencies among the peasants might prove fatal, turning our development definitely in the direction of capitalism. On the contrary, were the State, i.e. socialist economy, to prevail in the general economic life of the country, then a more or less considerable 'liberation' of individualistic tendencies among the peasantry would enter the channel of a definite correlation of forces and would become purely a matter of expediency, resolving itself into such questions as how? when? for how long?

To put it differently, if the productive forces at the disposition of the socialist state and securing all the commanding heights, grow not only rapidly, but more rapidly than the individualistic, capitalistic productive forces of the town and the rural districts, and if this is proved by the experience of the most difficult period of reconstruction, it becomes clear that a certain expansion of the individualistic commercial tendencies, springing from the very core of peasant agriculture, in no way threatens us with any economic surprises, with a precipitate change of quality and quantity, that is to say, with a sharp turn to capitalism.

Lastly, comes the third question, regarding the rate of our development from the standpoint of world economy. At a first glance, it would seem that this question, despite its importance, was a subsidiary one; we might argue, of course, that it is desirable to attain socialism 'as soon as possible', but once the movement is secured by the victorious development of socialist tendencies under the conditions of the New Economic Policy, the question of the rate of development assumes, as it were, a position of secondary importance. This is, however, not true. Such a conclusion would be correct (and that not absolutely), if we possessed an independent and self-sufficient economic system. But this is not the case. It was particularly owing to our achievements that we entered the world market, that is to say, we became a part of the world system of labour division, while being surrounded by capitalism. Under these conditions, the rate of our economic development will determine the strength of our opposition to the economic pressure of world capital and to the military and political pressure of world imperialism. And for the time being we cannot leave these factors out of account.

If we approach the control figures of the State Planning Commission and the explanatory notes to them with our three 'control' questions, we will see that they provide not only a clear and comprehensive, but a highly favourable reply to the two first questions, relating to the development of our productive forces and the social forms of this development. As regards the third question, concerning the rate of our development in the course of our economic growth, we have only reached the point at which it can be raised in the internal scale. But here, as we shall see, a favourable reply to the two first questions creates the conditions also for a solution of the third. The solving of the last is the highest goal of our economic development in the near future.

III

That our productive forces have recovered rapidly is now a well-established fact. There is no greater proof of it than the table of control figures. The produce of agriculture in the financial year 1924-25, including the bad harvest of 1924, reckoned at pre-war prices, amounted to 71 per cent of the yield of the favourable agricultural year of 1913. The financial year of 1925-26 with its splendid harvest, according to the latest estimates, promises to exceed the figure of 1913 and to be only slightly below that of 1911. If our total collected supplies of grain in the last few years have never reached 3 milliard poods, it is estimated that in the present year they will yield 4.1.*

Our industries in the concluding year had, in regard to the value of their output, reached 71 per cent of the output of the full-blooded year of 1913. In the next financial year it is estimated that production will reach no less than 95 per cent of the 1913 figure, that is to say, it will practically have completed its process of recovery. If we remember that in the year 1920 our production had fallen to one-fifth or one-sixth of the productive capacity of our factories, we shall realize more clearly how rapid has been the process of our recovery. The output of the State industries has trebled since 1921. Our exports, which do not amount to half a milliard roubles in the current year, promise to exceed a milliard in the next. Our imports too, are showing a like development. The State Budget from 2½ milliard roubles promises to go far beyond 3½ milliard roubles. Such are the principal control figures. The quality of our manufactures, still very imperfect, it is true, has nevertheless shown great improvement since the first two years of the New Economic Policy. Thus, to the question as to whether our productive forces are developing, we receive the emphatic reply — the 'emancipation' of the market has given a most powerful impulse to the productive forces.

But the fact that the impulse has come from the market — a factor of a capitalist order — has stimulated and still stimulates the malice of theoreticians and politicians, the bourgeoisie. The nationalization of industry and planned methods of economy seemed to have become hopelessly compromised by the fact of our recourse to the New Economic Policy and its undoubted economic success. And it is only an answer to our second question regarding the social forms of our economy, that can provide a socialist evaluation of our development.

* These are the estimates of today (August 28, 1925). The figures may, of course, vary one way or the other.

The productive forces of Canada are growing, for instance, stimulated by capital from the United States. In India the productive forces develop notwithstanding the throes of Colonial oppression. Productive forces too, are growing in the form of reconstruction, in the Germany of the Dawes Commission. But all these are cases of capitalist development. In Germany particularly, all plans for nationalization and socialization which had been so popular — at least in the fat books of academic socialists and among Kautsky's followers — during 1919 and 1920, have been cast aside like so much rubbish, while under the hard patronage of America, the principle of private capitalist enterprise, in spite of the teeth that have fallen out, is celebrating its second youth. How do matters stand with us in this regard? What social form is the development of our productive forces assuming? Are we marching towards socialism or towards capitalism?

A premise of a socialist economy is the nationalization of the means of production. Has this premise survived the test of the New Economic Policy? Has the commercial method of distribution of commodities led to the weakening or the strengthening of nationalization?

The control figures of the State Planning Commission provide unique material for the estimation of the reciprocal action and the struggle between socialist and capitalist tendencies in our economic system. We have here indisputable 'control' figures which cover basic capital, production, trade, capital and all the other important economic processes of the country.

The most conditional among the figures are probably those relating to the distribution of basic capital, but this has a far greater bearing on the intrinsic (absolute) value of the figures than on their mutual relation, and we are much more interested in the latter. According to the estimation of the State Planning Commission, at the commencement of the financial year, the State owned capital funds 'on a most modest reckoning' of no less than 11.7 milliard *chervontzi* roubles, the co-operatives 0.5 milliard roubles and individuals — mostly peasant agricultural holdings — 7.5 milliard roubles. This signifies that 62 per cent of the whole means of production has been socialized, including those with the best technical equipment. Only 38% remains non-socialized property.

As regards agriculture, the figures so far show results not so much of the nationalization of the land, as of the liquidation of landlordism. The results are both serious and instructive. The liquidation of land-

lordism and all landownership but that of the peasants, has brought
about the liquidation of the big estates, among which were some of the
most up-to-date farms. This was one of the reasons, a secondary one,
it is true, of the temporary decline of agriculture. But we know now
that the harvest of the present year is raising agriculture to the pre-war
standard without landlordism and without capitalist 'scientifically-
run' farms. And we are only at the commencement of the development of agriculture, entirely free from landlordism! This means that
the elimination of the landlord class with all its 'nests' and even the
'barbaric black partition' — meaning the transfer of the whole land to
the peasants — which had so alarmed the respectable Mensheviks, has
already justified itself in the economy as a whole. This is a first, and
we might say, not unimportant result.

Regarding the nationalization of the land, owing to the large
number of peasant holdings, it has been impossible, so far, to estimate
its results. The early period of socialization inevitably assumed a rosy
'for the people' hue, the gilt edge of which, as inevitably, fell away
from it after a while. At the same time, the idea of nationalization as a
socialist measure under a government of the working class has sufficiently maintained itself to make us understand its great importance
in the future development of agriculture. Through the nationalization
of the land, we have secured for the Government unlimited opportunities for a land policy. No individual or group property in our
country, will stand in the way of the adoption of forms of utilization of
the land for the needs of production. At the present moment, the
productive means of agriculture are nationalized to the extent of 4 per
cent, the remaining 96 per cent still being in the private ownership of
the peasants. We must bear in mind, however, that the agricultural
means of production, both of the peasants and of the State, form but a
little over a third of all the means of production of the Soviet Union. It
is hardly necessary to say that the full importance of the nationalization of the land will only be felt when agriculture has attained a high
technical standard, resulting in collective cultivation of the land, that
is to say, many years hence. But this is the direction along which we
are progressing.

IV

For us Marxists it was, of course, clear even before the Revolution,
that a socialist reconstruction of the economy would commence with
industry and transport, and then proceed to agriculture. For this

reason a statistical survey of the activities of the nationalized industries becomes the key-stone of the socialistic valuation of the present transitional economy.

In industry the means of production have been socialized to the extent of 89 per cent, including the railways to 97 per cent; the means of production in the big industries have been socialized to the extent of 99 per cent. These figures show that as regards property, the results of nationalization during these years have not changed to the prejudice of the Government. This circumstance alone is of great importance. But what concerns us chiefly is something else. What percentage of socialized means of production is included in the yearly output? That is to say, to what degree of productivity has the Government utilized the means of production it has appropriated to itself? The control figures of the State Planning Commission give us the following answer to this question: the national and co-operative industries have, in the financial year 1923-1924, turned out 76.3 per cent of the whole volume of products; in the present year, 79.3 per cent and in the next year, according to the control estimates of the StatePlanning Commission, they promise to turn out 79.7 per cent. As regards private industry, the output of the latter in the year1923-24, has equalled 23.7 per cent; in 1924-25, 20.7 per cent, and in the next year the amount estimated is 20.3 per cent. Apart from the cautious provisional estimate for the next year, a comparison of the growth of national and private output in the aggregate volume of goods in the country, is of the utmost importance. We see that in the past and present year, that is to say, in the years of intensive economic development, the proportion of state industries has grown by 3 per cent, and private industries have decreased to the same amount. This percentage, for the short period in question, marks the growing strength of socialism as against capitalism. The percentage may appear insignificant, but as a matter of fact, its symptomatic importance is enormous.

Wherein lay the danger of the transition to the New Economic Policy in the early years of its adoption? It lay in the fact that owing to the complete exhaustion of the country the State might not have been strong enough to lift on its shoulders in so short a time the big industrial undertakings. Their reduced capacity (the capacity of the industries had fallen to 10 and 20 per cent of former days) gave to the smaller, petty, and even the home industries the enormous advantage of greater mobility. The so-called 'selling out' of the early revolutionary period, which was the socialist payment to capitalism for restarting the factories and works confiscated from it, threatened to deliver into the hands of merchants, middlemen and speculators, a big part of the national property. The home industries and small workshops were the first to revive in the atmosphere of the New Economic Policy. A combination of private commercial capital with the petty and home industries might have resulted in a rapid process of the accumulation of private wealth along well-trodden roads. These conditions threatened such a loss of speed in the rate of development that the economic leadership might have been snatched from the hands of the workers' State. We do not, of course, mean to say by this that every temporary or protracted increase in the strength of private industry in the aggregate turnover, inevitably threatens catastrophic or even trying consequences. Even here, quality depends upon quantity. If the control figures had shown us that the strength of private capitalist production for the last two or three years had increased by one, two, or three per cent, this would not have meant that a dangerous position had been created; State production would still have consisted of three-fourths of the aggregate volume, and the recovery of the speed lost now, when the big undertakings are working at increasing rate of capacity, would have been a problem possible of solution. Had we been shown that the proportion of private capitalist production had increased by five or ten per cent, serious account would have had to be taken of the fact, but even then, for the early period of reconstruction, it would not have meant that economically nationalization was a disadvantage. We should only have seen that the major part of the nationalized industries had not yet embarked on the necessary process of development. The fact assumes greater significance in that during the early, purely reconstructive period of the New Economic Policy — a difficult and dangerous period for the Government — the nationalized industries had not only not ceded any of their functions to the capitalist industries, but had, on the contrary, succeeded in squeezing the latter out to the extent of 3 per cent. Such is the symptomatic significance of this small figure.

The issue becomes clearer if we examine the figures concerning not only production but the trade turnover. In the first six months of 1923, the proportion of private capital in trade was about 50 per cent; in the last six months it was 34 per cent; in 1924-25, about 26 per cent. In other words the importance of private capital in trade for these two years had decreased by half (from one-half to one-quarter). The result was in no way attained by the hampering of trade, for during the same period State and Co-operative trade had increased by more than half their former volume. Thus we see the decline not only of private industry, but also of private trade. And the one and the other have come about as a result of the fundamental growth of the productive forces and the increase in the trade turnover. For the coming year, the control figures estimate a further decrease — a slight one, it is true — in the weight of private industry and trade. We may await without much misgiving the realization of this prediction. The victory of State industry over private industry need not necessarily be conceived as a single continually ascending line. There may be periods when the State, sure of its economic power and desirous of increasing the rate of development, purposely allows a temporary increase in the weight of private enterprise — in agriculture in the shape of capitalist farms; in industry and in agriculture too, in the form of concessions. Taking into consideration the split-up condition of the major part of our private industries, it would be naive to imagine that every increase in the weight of private production above the present 20.7 per cent, would mean an inevitable danger to socialist construction. It would be altogether wrong to attempt to establish a hard and fast line of percentage in this respect. The question is determined not by a formal line, but by the general dynamics of development. A study of the latter shows that in the most difficult period, when the big undertakings showed their negative sides rather than their positive, the State withstood with full success the first onslaught of private capital. During the rapid development of the last two years, the correlation of economic forces created by the revolutionary upheaval has systematically advanced in favour of the Government. Now, when the position is consolidated by the very fact that the big industries have begun to work to 100 per cent of their capacity, there can be no ground for the fear of unexpected events, at any rate in regard to the domestic factors of our economy.

V

With regard to 'contract', that is to say, to the combined economic work of town and rural districts, the control figures give the most important and hence the most convincing particulars.*

---

* In this and in other instances I do not mean to imply that all the particulars of the table of control figures are new, but that they have been verified, renewed and included in a system embracing the whole of the national economy. This is what makes them so interesting.

The control figures show us that the peasantry place on the market less than a third of their total produce and that this volume of commercial agricultural produce forms over a third of the whole of the trade turnover.

The value of the industrial and marketed agricultural commodities constitute approximately 63 and 37 per cent. This means that should goods be measured not by the piece, pood, arshin (28 inches), but in roubles, a little over a third of the goods turnover would be the commodities of the rural districts and a little under two thirds those of the town. This is due to the fact that the rural districts satisfy their own needs to a large extent outside the market, while the towns place nearly all their produce on the market. More than two-thirds of the consumption of the scattered peasant holdings is excluded from the market, and only the lesser third has an influence on the economy of the country. Industry, on the contrary, by its very nature, directly participates with the whole of its products in the total national turn-over, for the 'natural' turnover within industry itself (through the trusts and syndicates), while decreasing the commercial produce by 11 per cent, not only does not decrease, but by simplifying the turnover, increases the importance of industry in the general economic process. However, if the 'naturally' consumed volume of agricultural produce has no influence on the market, it does not necessarily mean that it has no influence on the economy. Under given economic conditions it forms the necessary base for the commercial third of peasant production. This third, in its turn, forms the value for which the rural districts demand the equivalent from the towns. Hence, the gigantic economic importance of peasant production as a whole, and its commercial third in particular, becomes clear. The realization of crops, and more particularly export operations, enter as major factors into the annual economic balance sheets. The further we proceed the more does the machinery of exchange become complicated. The question is not limited by a long way to the exchange of a given number of poods of peasant grain for a given number of arshins of printed cotton. Our economic system has become part of the world system. This has made new links in the chain of exchange. Peasant grain is exchanged for foreign gold. Gold is exchanged for machinery, implements and other requisite articles of consumption for town and village. Textile machinery acquired for gold and paid for by the export of grain, provides new equipment for the textile industry and thus lowers the prices of fabrics sent to the rural districts. The circle becomes very complicated, but the basis remains the same — a certain economic relation between town and village.

We must not for a moment forget, however, that this relation is dynamic, and that in this complicated dynamic process, *the directing principle is industry*. This means that if agricultural production, and more particularly its commercial volume, marks out certain boundaries for the development of industry, these boundaries need not necessarily be hard and fast ones. It means that it is possible for industry to expand, not merely to the extent of the increase in crops, but beyond it. Leaning chiefly with its light flank on rural production and developing by its growth, industry increases in power as a market for its own needs.

At the present moment when agriculture and industry are completing their process of recovery, the motive power of progress will belong more than ever to industry. The problem of the socialist influence of the town over the rural districts by the supply to the villages not only of cheap articles, but of the more perfected agricultural implements requiring collective methods of work, now confronts industry in all its concrete reality and vastness. Agriculture will be reconstructed on socialist lines through the medium of co-operation not merely as a bare system of organization, but through co-operation plus scientific methods of cultivation, electrification and technical improvements generally. This means that the technical and socialistic progress of agriculture are inseparable from the growing preponderance of industry in the economic life of the country.

VI

The output of industry for the year 1924-25, has exceeded the output of the previous year by 48 per cent. Next year an increase of 33 per cent over the present year is anticipated, that is, if we leave a possible drop in prices out of consideration. The different industrial enterprises are not by any means developing at the same rate.

The big enterprises have grown in the present year by 64 per cent. The second group, which we might conditionally term the medium enterprises, have grown by 55 per cent; the small enterprises have increased their output only by 30 per cent. We have consequently reached conditions when the predominance of the big enterprises over the medium and small is very strongly manifested. This, however, does not mean that we have achieved all the possibilities of the socialist economy. In relation to the greater output of the big enterprises as compared with the medium and the small, we are only achieving that predominance of big enterprises which they have even under capitalism. The standardization of products on an all-national scale, a rationalization of the productive processes, a specialization of enterprises, the conversion of whole factories into huge parts of one single manufacturing body of the entire Union, a constructive linking-up of the productive processes of all the branches of industry, both in the raising of raw material and manufacturing — these are the fundamental industrial problems of socialism which we are only commencing to approach. Here, there open up immeasurable possibilities, which in the course of a few years might enable us to advance far beyond our old standard. This is, however, a problem of the future and we will examine it later on.

Up to now we have used the advantages of the State management of the economy not in production itself, that is to say, in the organization of its material processes, but in regard to industrial distribution — in the supply of the different industries with raw materials, equipment and so on, or, to use commercial language, in supplying the floating and in part, the basic capital. Unfettered by the limitation of private property, the State has been able through the State Budget, the State Bank, the Industrial Bank, etc., to direct the available resources where they were most needed for the reconstruction or development of the economic process. This advantage of socialist management has actually saved us in the past years. Notwithstanding the often grave miscalculations and mistakes in the distribution of resources, we have nevertheless distributed them incomparably more rationally and economically than would have been the case under an unrestricted capitalist process of recovery of productive forces. This alone has enabled us in so short a space of time to attain our present standard without foreign loans. But this does not exhaust the question. The economy, and, consequently, the expediency of socialism was manifested in the fact that it had freed the process of economic recovery from the additional charge of the up-keep of parasitic classes. We have reached a position when we are approximating to the productive standard of 1913, while the country is considerably poorer than it was before the war. This means that we are attaining corresponding productive results without the burden of the upkeep of a monarchy, a nobility, a bourgeoisie, ultra-privileged intellectual classes, and last-ly, without the obstructive friction of the capitalist machine itself.* It was owing to this socialist method in particular that we were able, with the limited means at our disposal, to mobilize much more of them for productive purposes, thereby preparing for a more rapid growth in the standard of life of the population in the next stage of our development.

*   *   *

Thus, from the nationalized land, cultivated in small-holdings by the peasants, we have commercial produce consisting of a little over a third of the goods turnover. The socialized capital of agriculture barely reaches 4 per cent.

We have industries, the socialized basic capital of which equals 89 per cent, supplying over 79 per cent of the total industrial products. The 11 per cent of the non-socialized means of production consequently turn out over 20 per cent of the total products.† The proportion of State industries is thus seen to be growing.

The railways are nationalized to the extent of 100 per cent. The work of transport is continually expanding. In the year 1921-22, it formed about 25 per cent of the pre-war figure; in 1922-23, 37 per cent; in 1923-24, 44 per cent, and, finally, in 1924-25, it will form over half the pre-war figure. The freight-turnover for next year is estimated at 75 per cent of the pre-war figure.

---

* Deposit and current account in the year 1924-25 averaged no more than 11 per cent of the 1913 figure. By the end of next year it is estimated that they will increase to 36 per cent. This is one of the striking indication of the small amount of our savings. But it is particularly the fact that while our deposit and current accounts formed only 11 per cent of the pre-war we have been able to bring our industries to almost three-fourths of the pre-war standard that shows that the workers' and peasants State has utilized the public resources more economically and rationally than a brougeois regime.

The slower development of transport in comparison with agriculture and industry is due to the fact that before the war the weight of exports and imports was considerably greater than it is now. This again shows that we are approaching the pre-war standard in industry with much lesser national resources and less public expenditure than in 1913.

† This dissimilarity in the means of production and in production itself, is due mainly to the difference in the organic composition of capital. Naturally, equipment in the small and home industries is insignificant compared to the manpower, which is not taken into account. To this must be added the fact that our big enterprises, such, for instance, as the big metallurgical industries, are, by a long way, not yet working to their full capacity.

As regards trade, the socialized, that is to say, the State and Co-operative resources, form about 70 per cent of the aggregate capital turnover, and this proportion is continually increasing.

Foreign trade has been socialized completely; the State monopoly of it is the solid foundation of our economic policy. The aggregate turnover of foreign trade is expected to increase in the next year to 2,200,000,000 roubles. The proportion of private capital represented in this turnover, even including contraband goods, which should be included, will hardly reach 5 per cent.

The banks and the entire credit system have been socialized practically by 100 per cent. And this vast and expanding machinery is growing more and more capable of mobilizing the financial resources for the needs of the productive processes.

The State Budget has increased to 3.7 milliard roubles, forming 13 per cent of the aggregate national income (29 milliard roubles), or 24 per cent of the goods volume (15,200,000,000 roubles). The Budget is becoming more and more a powerful lever for the raising of the economic and cultural life of the country.

Such are the control figures of the State Planning Commission.

*   *   *

These figures have a universal historic significance. More than a century of continuous activity on the part of socialists, commencing with Utopias and passing to scientific theory, has at last given birth to a great economic experiment, which has been going on for almost eight years. All that has been written regarding socialism and capitalism, freedom and oppression, dictatorship and democracy, has passed through the furnace of the October Revolution and Soviet economic experiment, and appears before us in a new, incomparably more concrete form. The figures of the State Planning Commission work out — it may be roughly and provisionally — the first sum total of the first chapter of the great experiment of the transition from a bourgeois to a socialist community. And this sum total is in favour of socialism.

No country has been so ruined and exhausted by a series of wars as Soviet Russia. All capitalistic countries which had suffered most from the War have, without exception, recovered by the help of foreign capital. It was only the land of the Soviets, the most backward in the past, the most ruined and exhausted by wars and the revolutionary upheaval, that has risen from complete poverty by her own efforts, surrounded by the active opposition of the entire capitalistic world. It is owing to the complete elimination of landlordism and bourgeois ownership of property, it is owing to the nationalization of all the principal means of production, it is owing to the State socialist methods of the mobilization and distribution of the essential resources, that the Soviet Union has risen from chaos, and as an ever-growing factor, is penetrating the world economic system. From the control figures of the State Planning Commission there stretch unbreakable threads to the past, to the Manifesto of the Communist Party of Marx and Engels, and also to the future — to the Socialistic future of humanity. The spirit of Lenin pervades these columns of dry figures.

CHAPTER TWO

We and the capitalist world

The attainment of the pre-war standard, both of quality and quantity, under existing historical conditions, will be a gigantic achievement. To this question our first chapter was devoted. But this achievement brings us only to the 'start' of our actual economic competition with world capitalism.

The concluding lines of the explanatory notes of the State Planning Commission formulate the following general programme: 'To hold on firmly to the conquered positions and every year to advance successively towards socialism, if only *a step at a time*, whenever economic conditions make it possible.' Taken literally, these lines might induce false conclusions. To advance towards socialism every year 'a step at a time' may be taken to mean that the rate of advance is unimportant — once the wind is set towards socialism, we shall get there anyhow. Such a conclusion would be fundamentally wrong; the State Planning Commission never meant the words to be taken in that light. As a matter of fact, the whole question lies in the rate of advance. It was only because State industry and trade developed more rapidly than private enterprise that the socialist equilibrium was achieved in the period we have passed through. A like relation must be preserved in the future. But what is still more important is the rate of our development as compared to the development of the world economy. The explanatory notes of the State Planning Commission have not so far touched on this question. Consequently, it is the more necessary for us to consider it, as this new standard will serve as a means of measuring our successes and failures of the near future, just as 'the pre-war standard' has done in the past, during the period of reconstruction.

It is evident that with our inclusion in the world market not only our opportunities will grow, but our dangers likewise. The dangers all come from the same source — the split-up condition of peasant agriculture, the technical backwardness of our industries, and the still great industrial preponderance over us of world capital. This simple admission of fact does not imply that the socialist regime with its socialist methods of production and its tendencies and possibilities are not stronger than those of capitalism. A lion is stronger than a dog, but an old dog may be stronger than a young lion cub. The best insurance for a young lion cub is to grow up and to have strong teeth and sharp claws. This only requires time.

What, particularly, makes old capitalism so far prevail over young socialism? It is not because of the riches it possesses, nor the gold it keeps in cellars, nor the volume of accumulated and stolen wealth. Past accumulations of wealth may have their importance, but they are not the determining factors. A living society cannot exist on old accumulations; it feeds on the products of living labour. Despite all her riches, ancient Rome could not withstand the onslaught of the 'barbarians', when they developed a higher productive capacity than that of her decaying regime of slavery. The bourgeois society of France, roused by the Great Revolution, simply looted the wealth accumulated from the Middle Ages by the aristocratic town communities of France. Were output in America to fall below the European standard, the nine milliards of gold kept in the cellars of her banks, would not help her. The economic superiority of bourgeois states lies in the fact that so far capitalism produces cheaper goods than socialism and of a better quality. In other words, the output, so far, is still much higher in countries living by the inertia of old capitalist civilization than in a country which has only just begun to adopt socialist methods under inherited uncivilized conditions.

We know the fundamental law of history — in the end that regime will conquer which ensures human society a higher economic standard. The historic contest can be decided not immediately, and not at a single stroke, only by the comparative coefficients of output.

The crux of the problem is this: in what direction and to what extent will the comparative value of our economy and the capitalist economy change within the next few years? We can compare them in various ways. Capitalist economies are by nature multiform. Comparison may be static, that is to say, it may proceed from the economic position of the actual moment, and dynamic, based on a comparison of the rates of development. We can compare the national income of capitalist countries with our own. And we can compare the coefficients of productive development. All these comparisons have varying degrees of importance; all we need is to comprehend their relation and dependence on one another. Below we give some examples — only to illustrate our meaning, nothing more.

In the United States of America the capitalist process has reached its highest point. To estimate the actual material supremacy of capitalism as compared with socialism, it is instructive to analyse it at its highest.

The council of the congress of American industries has recently issued a table from which we will quote a few figures. The population of the United States, which forms about 6 per cent of the population of the globe, produces about 21 per cent of the grain, 32 per cent of other cereals, 52 per cent of the cotton, 53 per cent of the wood products, 62 per cent of the cast iron, 60 per cent of the steel, 57 per cent of the paper, 60 per cent of the brass, 46 per cent of the lead, and 72 per cent of the oil of the world. The United States own a third of the world's wealth. America possesses about 38 per cent of the hydraulic power of the world, 59 per cent of the telegraphic communication and telephone wires, 40 per cent of all the railways, and 90 per cent of the motor vehicles.

The generating power of our electrical stations for public supply will reach 775,000 kilowatt in the coming year; last year this supply in America reached 15,000,000 kilowatt. The generating power of our electrical stations for industrial supply, according to the returns of 1920, was 1,000,000 kilowatt; in the United States for the same year, it was 10,500,000 kilowatt.

The total output is expressed in the national income, the estimation of which, as we know, presents great difficulties. According to the figures of our Central Statistic Board, the national income of the Soviet Union for the year 1923-24, averaged 100 roubles per head; in the United States of America the average is 550 roubles per head. Foreign statisticians, however, put the figure not at 550, but at 1,000 roubles per head. This means that output conditioned by equipment, organization, custom, etc., is, on an average, ten times, or at least six times higher in the United States than it is with us.

These figures, important as they are, in no way determine our defeat in the historic contest; not only because the capitalist system is

not limited to America, nor because there are forces engaged in the
struggle which have been generated by preceding economic development, but because, in the first place, the future curve of economic
development in America herself is an unknown quantity. The productive forces of the United States are not utilized to their fullest capacity,
by a long way, and non-utilization of the productive capacity means a
lowering of the productiveness of labour. The United States are not
assured of markets by a long way. The problem of selling confronts
them in all its acuteness. It is quite within the bounds of possibility
that in the near future productivity on either side will be equalized by
an increase in our own productiveness and a decrease in that of
America. To a much greater extent does this apply to Europe, the
productive standard of which is considerably lower than that of
America.

One thing is clear; the superiority of capitalist technical science and
economics is still enormous; the ascent before us is steep; the problems and difficulties are truly vast. To find a way and to mark it out is
only possible with the measuring instruments of world economics in
our hands.

The comparative coefficients of the world's economy

The dynamic equilibrium of the Soviet economy is not in any sense
the equilibrium of a self-contained and self-sufficient whole. On the
contrary, as time goes on, internal economic equilibrium will become
more and more dependent on export and import. This circumstance
must be fully examined, and every possible conclusion drawn from it.
The more we become part of the system of international division of
labour, the more directly will such elements of our domestic
economy, as prices and the quality of our goods, become dependent
on the corresponding elements of the world market.

Up to the present day, we have been developing our industries with
the pre-war standard always before us. For all comparisons and the
determination of values of our production, we use the price lists of
1913. But now that the early reconstruction period when such comparison, though imperfect, but admissible, is coming to an end, *the
whole question of gauges for our economic development has moved on to a
new plane*. Henceforth, we must know definitely at any given moment
to what extent our production, in quantity, quality and price, is
behind the production of the European or world market. The close of

the reconstruction period will definitely permit us to throw aside our own 1913 catalogues, and to arm ourselves with the present-day catalogues of German, English, American and other firms. We shall have to deal with new indices, expressing the comparison of our production, both in quality and price, with those of the world market. These new gauges, these new coefficients, not on a national but on a world scale, will be the only ones competent to register the different stages of the process described by Lenin in his formula — 'Who is going to score?'

★   ★   ★

In the antagonistic conditions of the world economy and world politics all depends on the rate of our development, that is to say, the rate of the quantitative and qualitative growth of our output. Today our backwardness and poverty is an undoubted fact, which we do not deny, but emphasize in every way. A systematic comparison with the world economy will therefore only bear this out in plain figures. Is there not a danger in the near future that we shall have barely risen firmly to our feet when the world market will crush us by the immense superiority of its natural resources? To a question thus put, there can be no definite, incontestable answer, particularly in figures, as there can be none to the question as to whether individualistic tendencies in farming (of the rich and greedy peasants) will not tempt the smaller holders, thus paralysing the ascendency of the proletariat over the peasants and creating political obstacles to socialist development. Similarly it would be impossible to give a categorical answer to the question as to whether capitalism will succeed — should its temporary and very relative tenacity continue to mobilize against us serious armed forces and by means of a new war check our economic progress. Here the problem is one of struggle, where creativeness, manoeuvring, energy and such-like factors play an enormous and sometimes decisive part. Examination of these questions does not enter into the scope of the present work, in which we are attempting to determine the inner tendencies of economic development, separating them as far as possible from other factors.

Anyhow, in reply to the question as to whether the world market would not crush us by its superior economic weight, we may say that we are not by any means defenceless; our economy is safeguarded by special national institutions, adopting an all round system of socialist protection. How far, however, is this system efficacious? This we may find out from the history of capitalist development. For long periods, Germany and the United States of America industrially lagged behind England, to such an extent which seemed insurmountable. Natural and historic circumstances later permitted these backward countries, under the cover of protective tariffs, to overtake and even to pass the country ahead of them. National boundaries, national power, and tariff systems were powerful factors in the history of capitalist development. This applies in a much greater degree to a socialist country. A carefully conceived, persevering and adaptable system of socialist protection becomes more important for us as our relations with capitalist markets become more extensive and involved.

It need hardly be said, however, that protection expressed at its highest in our foreign trade monopoly, is not all-powerful. Protection makes it possible to withstand the pressure of the volume of goods from capitalist countries by regulating it in accordance with the requirements of home production and consumption. In this way protection is able to ensure socialist industries the period necessary for raising their productive standard. Without a monopoly of foreign trade, our reconstructive process would be impossible, but, on the other hand, it is only our actual productive achievements which permit us to maintain a system of socialist protection. Later on also the monopoly of foreign trade while safe-guarding our home industries from foreign impacts which they are not yet strong enough to withstand, will not be able, of course, to take the place of the actual expansion of industry itself, which will henceforth be measured against the coefficients of the world market.

At present, our comparison with the pre-war standard relates only to quantity and prices. A product is taken, not for its consistency, but for its name. This, of course, is wrong. Comparative industrial coefficients must embrace questions of quality. Failing this, they may become sources and instruments of self-deception. In this connection we have had experience of reduced prices which in some cases have been counterbalanced by a lowering of quality. Given uniformity of quality in a particular commodity of our own and foreign production, the comparative coefficient is determined by the difference of cost price. Given the same cost price, the coefficient is determined by the difference in quality. Lastly, given a different cost price and quality, the valuation of the one and the other must be combined. To ascertain the cost price is a matter of industrial calculation. The quality of a commodity is ascertained, as a rule, with the help of several factors. A classic example is the electric lamp, the quality of which is determined by the length of time it serves, the amount of power it uses, and the evenness of its light distribution.

The establishment of definite technical norms and productive standards, including standards of 'quality', considerably simplifies the working out of the comparative coefficients. The relation between our standards and the standards of the world market will be a constant quantity for each given period of time. All we need to know is whether our product comes up to the established standard. As regards value comparisons, when once the relative qualities have been ascertained, the question is easily solved. A combined coefficient is arrived at by means of simple multiplication. If some commodity of ours were to be twice inferior to a foreign commodity and one and a half times dearer, the comparative coefficient would be one third.

To say that we do not know foreign cost prices is true, but is of secondary importance to the matter under consideration. It is enough for us to know the price quoted in the catalogue. The difference between the cost price and the selling price constitutes profit. A reduction of our own cost prices will enable us to make our selling prices level with those of the world market, irrespective of foreign cost prices. This will be in substance a solution of the vital question of the coming period. After that, a third period will commence — not immediately, it is true — the task of which will be to replace capitalist products on the world market with the products of socialist economies.

It is sometimes objected that the number of commodities is so great that the working out of the comparative coefficients is an 'insuperable' task. To this we may give a two-fold reply. In the first place, all commodities, no matter of what kind, form part of a calculation, and are entered into books and catalogues, and there is nothing insuperable in these tasks, despite the large number of commodities involved. In the second place, it is possible to limit ourselves in the beginning to the most important articles of mass consumption, the junction articles of each manufacture, so to speak, assuming that the remaining articles occupy the intermediate place in the system of comparative prices.

Another objection is based on the difficulties of gauging or even determining the quality. As a matter of fact, what is it that determines the quality of cotton fabric? Is it the durability, the weight of cotton in a square yard, the fastness of colour, the attraction to the eye? The difficulty of gauging the quality of most articles cannot be denied.

Nevertheless, the problem is not insoluble. All that is necessary is that we should not approach it with preconceived absolute criteria. In regard to cotton fabric intended for the peasants' and workers' market, durability takes the first place, and fastness of colour the second. If we measure these two moments — and it is possible to do this by strictly objective methods — we obtain a main description of quality expressed in quantity. It is even easier and simpler to give an exact, that is to say, a quantitative expression to the comparative coefficients of our ploughs, our threshing-machines, our tractors, and similar implements of American manufacture. This question will, in the next few years, be as important for agriculture as the renewal of basic capital for industry. In the buying of a horse or a cow, the peasant himself determines (with remarkable accuracy!) the essential 'coefficients'. In the buying of a machine, he is almost helpless. Having burnt his fingers on a bad gear, he passes on his terror even to his neighbours at the buying of a machine. It is essential that a peasant should be quite sure what kind of machine he is buying. A Soviet threshing-machine should have its trade passport, which should form the basis of the comparative coefficient. The peasant would then know what he was buying and the State would know the relation between our product and the American.*

The idea of comparative coefficients, which, at first glance, may seem abstract and, perhaps, pedantic, is in actual fact very vital, and is literally forced out of the prevailing conditions of the economy, and even out of all the holes and crevasses of everyday life. Our present comparative coefficients, calculated in relation to the pre-war standard, also possess not only theoretical but practical foundations. Our mass consumer, having no access to statistical tables and price curves, uses his memory and refers also to that of his family with regard to consumption. A statistical table tells of definite percentages to the pre-war standard, arrived at almost entirely from the quantitative side, while the consumer's memory adds: 'Before the war,' (that is to say, the imperialist war) 'a pair of boots cost so many roubles, and lasted so many months.' Every time he buys a pair of boots, the comparative coefficient flashes across his mind. Every buyer makes

* In the foregoing illustration, we did not mean to imply that the idea of comparative coefficients is opposed by interested groups. On the contrary, our producers, workers engaged in national trade, co-operative and scientific institutes, are all very sympathetic towards the idea, which springs out of our whole economic development. Work in this direction has already been begun by means of a Special Conference on quality of production, and by our scientific institutes.

that calculation — be it the Leather Trust purchasing machinery from the Voronej or Kiev engineering works, or a peasant woman buying three yards of printed cotton in the market place, with the difference only that the Trust refers back to catalogues and ledgers, and the peasant woman to her memory. And it must be admitted that the comparative coefficients of the peasant woman, based on actual experience of life, are sounder than the coefficients of the Trust, calculated hurriedly, nearly always without regard to quality, and sometimes with some preconceived idea. Somehow or other, statistics, economic analysis, and the consumer's daily exercise of his memory have all arrived at the necessity of finding a starting point in the conditions of the pre-war economy.

This peculiar national limitation, with an eye always to the past, is now coming to an end. Our connection with the world market is even now sufficiently developed to induce at every step a comparison of our goods with foreign goods. And in accordance with the measure in which comparisons with the old will cease, as the remembrance of old products will fade from the mind, particularly among the younger generation, new comparisons will become more vivid, being based not on memory, but on the vital facts of daily life. Our business men, returning from abroad, bring with them proposals of definite firms for definite goods, as well as catalogues of different firms, not to mention their own personal experience as consumers. The question, unknown in the past year, as to the price at which an article is sold abroad, and how far its quality differs from a similar article of our own manufacture, is asked now on all sides. Visits abroad will increase in frequency. By one or another we must introduce our trust directors, factory and works managers, the best among our technical students, foremen, fitters and qualified workers to foreign industry, not all at once, of course, but in turn. The aim of visits of this kind would be to furnish the main body of our economists and industrialists with an opportunity of investigating at first hand every unfavourable 'comparative coefficient', in order the better to turn it to our own advantage.

It would be bureaucratic unimaginativeness to suppose that the process of orientation towards the West is limited to the leaders of the economic life. On the contrary, the process is one of mass psychology, embracing in various ways the bulk of consumers. Contraband plays no small part in this respect and should not be disregarded. Contraband, though not commendable, still forms an actual part of economic life, being, moreover, based entirely on comparative coefficients of the world economy; a contrabandist brings into the country only those products of foreign manufacture which are cheaper and better than our own. The struggle for the improvement of the quality of our products, by the way, thus becomes the surest way of combating contraband, which is now sending millions of gold currency out of the country. Contraband flourishes mostly on small articles, but it is the very smallness of the wares which causes them the more readily to penetrate into the pores of our daily life.*

There is one more branch of industry which has never ceased to be compared with foreign production, and that is agricultural machinery and implements. The peasant used to be familiar with the Austrian scythe, and always compared it with our own. He knew the American MacCormick, the Canadian Harris, the Austrian Heid, and others. Now that agriculture is developing and there is a new demand for agricultural machinery and implements, these comparisons are reviving with the addition of the fresh comparison of the American Ford with our own make. When a peasant buys a horse-threshing-machine and the inferior iron gear wears away in a few hours before his eyes, he registers the fact in his mind with a very high coefficient of profanity indeed.

As regards the industrial worker, the latter is brought up against the comparative coefficient, not by the things he produces, but by those he uses for production and in part for consumption. He knows the quality of American and Russian lathes, instruments, cast iron, measuring instruments, etc. It need hardly be said that a well-qualified worker understands the question of quality very well, and that one of the tasks of an industrial education is to make him understand all the more.

Enough, we think, has been said to show that the comparative coefficients of world production are not figments of our imagination, but a practical question of greatest importance, reflecting the new problems of our economic development.

Such a system of comparative economics today would give us the present-day cross-section of our economy in the light of the achievements of world economy. Arriving at an average coefficient of all products would mean arriving at the exact degree of our backwardness in technical science and production. A periodic measuring of coefficients of goods and average coefficients would show us a picture

---

* A study of contraband goods is very important, both from the productive and national economic points of view.

of our achievements, and would gauge the rate at which we had arrived at them in the different branches of our industries and in industry as a whole.

Driving in a cart, we measure the miles by the eye or by hearsay; a motor-car has a speedometer. In the future our industries must advance with an international speedometer, the register of which shall be our guide, not only in the important economic measures we introduce, but also in many of our political decisions. If it is true that the success of a regime depends on increased production — and for us Marxists, this is an axiom — then an exact quantitative and qualitative measurement of the production of Soviet economics is needed, not only for present market purposes, but also in order to estimate the successive stages of the historic road we are following.

CHAPTER THREE

The rate of development and its material limitations and possibilities

In the years from 1922 to 1924 our general industrial revival was mainly dependent on the light industries. In the current financial year, predominance is passing to the branches of industry turning out implements of production. However, even the latter are reviving only to the extent of the utilization of old capital. During the coming financial year when the basic capital inherited from the bourgeoisie will be working to its full capacity, we shall commence extensive operations in the renewal of basic capital. The whole of the capital expenditure the State Planning Commission makes provision for amounts to 880,000,000 roubles on industry (including electrification); 236,000,000 roubles on transport, 365,000,000 roubles on housing and other buildings, 300,000,000 roubles on agriculture, making a total of over 1,800,000,000 roubles. The new capital included in this sum, that is to say the new savings of the whole economic system, amount to over 900,000,000 roubles. These provisional estimates, not yet finally revised, show a big advance in the distribution of the material resources of the country. Up to the present, we have been working on existing basic capital with small additions. In the future, we shall have to create new basic capital. This constitutes the fundamental difference between the coming economic period and that which is now passing.

In the view of individual business men, say directors of trusts, the rate of development may appear to correspond to the amount of credit obtainable from the banks. 'Give me so many millions and I'll put up a new roof, new lathes, increase output tenfold, halve cost prices, and bring quality up to European standard.' How many times have we heard this said! But the point is that financing is not the primary factor by a long way. The rate of economic development is determined by the material conditions of the productive process itself. This is very appropriately emphasized in the explanatory notes of the State Planning Commission. 'The universal limit of the possible rate of economic development,' it is said in the notes, 'a limit conditioning all the separate limiting factors, is the amount of national saving in material form, that is to say, the aggregate newly-created wealth which remains after having covered the needs of simple reproduction, thus forming a basis for extended reproduction and reconstruction.'

Bank-notes, shares, bonds, bills of exchange and other 'securities' do not matter in themselves in the scope and rate of our development; they are only auxiliary implements for the calculation and distribution of material values. Of course, from the individualistic, capitalist point of view, and the view of an individualistic economy in general, these securities have an independent importance of their own, for they ensure the possessor of a certain amount of material values. But from the national economic point of view, which in our conditions closely approximates to that of the State, securities in themselves add nothing to the actual volume of goods, which serves as a basis for the expansion of production. This actual basis, in consequence, must be our starting-point. The financial resources directed through the Budget, the banks, loans for economic reconstruction, the industrial fund and so on, are only a means of distributing among the various branches of the economy the corresponding material products.

Before the war, our industry developed, on an average, at the rate of 6 or 7 per cent annually. The coefficient, we must admit, is high. It seems negligible, however, when we compare it with the coefficients of the present day, when industry is expanding at the rate of 40 or 50 per cent annually. Nevertheless, it would be a stupid mistake simply to compare these two coefficients of growth. Up to the War, the expansion of industry consisted mainly in the building of new factories. At the present time, expansion consists to a much larger degree in the utilization of old works and old machinery. Hence we have this tremendous rate of growth. We must naturally expect that with the completion of the process of recovery, the coefficient of growth will be considerably reduced. This circumstance is of special importance, since it determines, to a considerable extent, our position in the capitalist world. The struggle for our socialist 'place in the sun' must inevitably become a struggle for the highest possible coefficient of productive growth. The basis, and at the same time, the 'limit' of this growth is, after all, the volume of material values.

But if this is the case, if the process of recovery re-creates, in fact, the old relationship between agriculture and industry, between the home and foreign market (the export of grain and raw materials, import of machinery and fabrics), does it not mean that it will also re-create the pre-war coefficient of growth, and that our present 40 to 50 per cent will fall to a pre-war 6 per cent? It is, of course, impossible to give a definite answer to this question. Nevertheless, we say with confidence that possessing a socialist state, nationalized industry and increasing regulation of the basic economic processes, including exports and imports, we can still maintain the coefficients of growth even after we have attained the pre-war standard, going far beyond the latter and the average coefficient of a capitalist country.

In what do our strong points consist? We have already enumerated them.

In the first place, we have practically no parasitic classes. Actual accumulation before the war amounted not to 6 per cent, but at least to twice as much per year. But only half of it was used productively, the other half being rapaciously wasted by parasitic classes. Thus, the mere abolition of the monarchy, the bureaucracy, the nobility and the bourgeoisie, given other necessary conditions, ensures us an increase in the co-efficient of growth of not 6 but of 12 per cent, or 9 to 10 per cent at least.

In the second place, the knocking down of individualist capitalist fences makes it possible for the State at any given moment to mobilize with perfect freedom the necessary resources required by any economic unit. Unproductive charges of parallel enterprises, competition, etc., have been largely eliminated and will be still further eliminated as time goes on. It was only owing to these circumstances that we have been able without foreign help to recover so quickly in the last few years. In future, the planned distribution of forces and resources alone will make it more possible to obtain greater productive results with the same expenditure of resources than would be possible in a capitalist community.

In the third place, the planning principle which we have barely commenced to introduce in the technical side of production (standardization, specialization of factories, the combination of factories into a single industrial organization) promises a serious and ever growing increase in the coefficient of our production in the near future.

In the fourth place, a capitalist community lives and develops by alternate periods of prosperity and crises, which in the years since the war have assumed a most unwholesome, spasmodic character. It is true that our economy is not free from crises either. Moreover, our growing contact with the world market, as we shall show later, is a possible source of crises in our own economy. Nevertheless, increased provision and regulation in the planning of production will considerably alleviate the periods of crises in our development, and thereby ensure additional accumulations of wealth.

Such are the four strong points which have already markedly influenced our development in the past years. Their import does not lessen; it will, on the contrary, grow with the conclusion of the process of recovery as a whole. If properly utilized, they will make it possible in the next few years to increase the coefficient of our industrial growth, not only doubling, but trebling the pre-war 6 per cent and perhaps going even beyond that.

This, however, does not exhaust the question. The advantages of socialist economy which we have enumerated will make their influence felt not only on the domestic economic processes; they will be greatly strengthened by the possibilities opened up by the world market. We have already examined the dangers resulting from the entry into the world market. The capitalist market, however, is not only fraught with dangers for us; it also opens up immense opportunities. It provides a widening access to the highest achievements of technical science and the most complex articles of production. The world market, drawing the socialist economy within its orbit, creates new dangers for socialism, but at the same time it gives to the socialist state which properly regulates its turnover, powerful means of countering these dangers. By a wise utilization of the world market we shall be able to a great extent to speed up the evolutionary process of the comparative coefficients to the advantage of socialism.

Of course, as we advance, we must strictly gauge the bed of the river, considering that this is the first passage of the socialist state across that river. But all the facts indicate that the farther we go, the deeper and broader will the channel become.

CHAPTER FOUR

Socialist development and resources of the world market

From the national economic standpoint as opposed to the individual economic standpoint, securities in themselves cannot accelerate productive development, just as the shadow of a person cannot add to his height. From the international economic point of view, however, the question appears quite different. American bank-notes in themselves cannot produce a single tractor, but should the Soviet Government possess a goodly amount of these, it would enable us to import tractors from the United States.

In relation to the world capitalist economy, the Soviet Government acts as a big private property owner; it exports its goods, imports foreign goods, uses credit, buys foreign technical support, and, finally, attracts private capital by the formation of mixed companies and the granting of concessions.

The 'restorative' process has also restored our position on the world market. We must not, therefore, forget for a moment the great mutual dependence which used formerly to exist between the economy of capitalist Russia and world capital. We must just bring to mind the fact that nearly two-thirds of the technical equipment of our works and factories used to be imported from abroad. This dependence has hardly decreased to any considerable extent in our own time, which means that it will scarcely be economically profitable for us in the next few years to produce at home the machinery we require, at any rate, more than two-fifths of the quantity, or at best, more than half of it. If we were suddenly to shift our resources and forces to the making of new machinery, we would either destroy the necessary proportion between the different branches of the economy and between the basic and circulating capital in a given branch, or, if we maintained the proportion, we should be greatly decreasing the whole coefficient of development. And for us, a decrease in the rate of development is infinitely more dangerous than the import of foreign machinery or of the foreign goods we require in general.

We make use of foreign technical science and foreign productive formulae. Our engineers, in increasing numbers, visit Europe and America, and those of them who are sharp-sighted bring away everything that can possibly speed up our economic development. We are now proceeding more and more by simply buying foreign technical assistance, as we tie up our trusts with outstanding foreign firms, which undertake to develop in our country in a stipulated time the production of particular commodities.

The great importance of foreign trade for our agriculture is evident. Mechanical methods, involving collective cultivation, will go hand in hand with the growth of export. In exchange for our agricultural produce we receive agricultural machinery or machinery for the production of agricultural machinery.

But the question is not only one of machinery. Every foreign product which is able to fill a certain gap in the system of our economy, be it raw material or a partly manufactured commodity, or an article of consumption, can, under certain conditions, help our economic work, increasing the rate of our development. Of course, the import of articles of luxury, articles of parasitic consumption, will only retard our development. But a timely import of one or other commodity of consumption, in so far as it serves to establish the necessary equilibrium on the market and to fill up the gap in the workers' or peasants' budget, will only accelerate our economic progress.

In our foreign trade, conducted by the State, adaptable and supplementary to the work of the State industries and home trade, we have a powerful means of speeding up our economic development. Of course, our foreign trade will become the more productive in results the greater the credit facilities it is able to create for itself on the world market.

What does foreign credit do for our economic development? Capitalism makes advances to us against our savings which do not yet exist, but which we are still to accumulate within one, two, or five years. As a result, the foundations of our development are extended beyond the limits of our actual savings of today. If by the help of

European technical formulae we are able to speed up the process of our production, we can speed it still more by the help of European or American machinery obtained on credit. The dialectics of historical development have resulted in capitalism becoming for a time the creditor of socialism. Well, has not capitalism been nourished at the breasts of feudalism? History has honoured the debt.

Concessions come into the same category. A concession combines the transfer to our country of foreign plant, foreign productive formulae, and the financing of our economy by the resources of world capitalist savings. Among the many branches of industry, concessions may and should be given the greatest importance. It is needless to say that the limits of our concessionary policy are the same as those in regard to all individualistic capitalistic forms of industry — the State retains the higher commands and carefully maintains the determining weight of the State industry over the concessionary. But within these limits, the concessionary policy still has extensive scope.

To the same kind, finally, belong, as a crowning of the whole system, possible State loans. A State loan is the purest form of advance against our future socialist savings. A loan of gold — the commodity of all commodities — enables us to buy abroad manufactured articles, raw materials, machinery, patents, and to engage the best instructors and engineers of Europe and America.

In all that has been said, we see the necessity for us of a more accurate, that is, more systematic and scientific orientation in all questions connected with the world economic turnover. What machinery to import? For what factories? When? What other goods to import and in what order? How to distribute the gold currency funds between the different branches of industry? What specialists to invite? To which branches of the economy to attract concessionary capital? On what scale? And for what period? It is quite evident that these questions cannot be decided from day to day, at a guess, upon the spur of some particular economic impetus. The minds of our workers in economic issues are obstinately, perseveringly and far from unsuccessfully, engaged in evolving methods of dealing with the questions enumerated above, and many more inseparably connected with them, the foremost of which is the question of export. The problem is one of preserving the proportion of progress between the main branches of industry and the economy as a whole by means of an opportune inclusion in the proportion of such elements of the world economy as will help to speed up development all round. For the settlement of various practical questions arising as a result of this in the elaboration of prospective plans for one year, five years or for longer periods, the system of comparative coefficients will be found to be of invaluable help. If in the main branches of industry the comparative coefficient is particularly unfavourable for us it will necessitate the import from abroad of ready-made commodities, patents, formulae, new plant; or we may apply to foreign specialists or invite foreign interests to take up concessions. The foreign policy and the concessions policy can only take the lead and be properly planned if based on a widely elaborated system of the comparative coefficients of industry.

The same methods will later be applied to the solution of the question of *the renewal of basic capital* and the extension of production. In what branches of industry to renew the plant first? What new factories to build? It is needless to say that wants and demands far exceed possibilities. In what way, then, are we to approach the question?

First of all, we must find out the exact amount of the savings available for the re-equipment of works and for the building of new factories. Our most urgent and vital needs we will cover with our own savings. If the way to other sources is closed to us, then domestic savings will determine the scope of the extension of our production.

Side by side with this, it is essential to establish a proper order for dealing with demands from the view of the needs of the economic process as a whole. In this respect the comparative coefficients will immediately indicate the branch of industry to which capital expenditure should be first applied.

Such, in the roughest outline, purposely evading a whole range of complex moments, is our transition to the planning principle in the solution of questions connected with the renewal and extension of the basic capital of industry.

CHAPTER FIVE

The socialization of the productive process

A State which possesses nationalized industries, a monopoly of foreign trade, the monopoly of attracting foreign capital to one or other branch of its economy, has at its disposal a vast arsenal of resources by means of which it can speed up the rate of economic development. All these resources, however, though resulting from the very nature of the socialist state, do not, as such, so far enter into the productive processes. In other words, had we preserved all the works and factories in their working order of 1913, their nationalization even under those conditions would have given us enormous advantages by a planned economical distribution of our resources.

The economic achievements of the reconstructive period are due largely to the socialist methods of productive distribution; that is to say, to the planned or semi-planned methods of providing the necessary resources to the different branches of the national economy. The possibilities resulting from our relations with the world market have also been examined mainly from the view of the means of production, and not from the inner organization of production.

We must not, however, for a moment forget that the fundamental advantages of socialism lie in the sphere of production itself. These advantages, utilized by us as yet but to a quite insignificant extent, open up infinite possibilities in the matter of speeding up the rate of our development. The first place must be accorded to actual nationalization of scientific technical thought and all industrial inventions; the centralized-planning solution of the problem of power for the economy as a whole and for each area in particular; the standardization of all products, and, lastly, the successive specialization of factories.

47

The work of scientific and technical thought are not fenced-off private property with us. Any achievement in organization and technology of any undertaking, any improvement in a chemical or other formula, immediately become the property of all the works and factories which are interested in it. Scientific and technical institutes are able to test ideas in any of the State undertakings, while every enterprise is at liberty, through the institutes, to utilize for its purposes, at any moment, the collective experience of industry as a whole. Scientific and technical thought is in principle socialized with us. In this respect, however, we have not yet done with conservative partitions, partly theoretical, partly material, which we have inherited with the nationalized property of the capitalists. We are only just learning how to make the most of the possibilities arising from the nationalization of scientific and technical discoveries. Along this line we might achieve untold advantages in the next few years, which would sum up in a result of the utmost value to us, that of speeding up the rate of our development.

Another source of great economy, and consequently of increased productivity of labour, is the sound management of power. The need for motive power is common to all branches of industry, all enterprises, the material activities of man in general. This means that motive power as a common multiplier may more or less be brought outside the brackets of all branches of industry. It is clear that we can achieve enormous economies by making away with all privately owned power, by separating it from the different works with which it was formerly connected only owing to private ownership and not for any reasons of technical, national or economic expediency.

The electrification scheme is only one part of the programme for the nationalization of fuel and power. Without the adoption of such a programme, the nationalization of the means of production would not bear its full fruit. Private property, abolished as a legal institution, is still retained in the organization of these enterprises, which form enclosed little worlds unto themselves. The problem is to make the principle of nationalization penetrate deeper and deeper into the productive process and into its material and technical conditions. We must nationalize motive power in fact. This refers to the existing power-producing plants and yet still more to those we are to create. The combine, Dneprstroy — which it is proposed to create as a combine uniting a powerful electrical station and a range of industries and transport bodies desiring cheap power — is already, in a technical sense, built on the principles of socialism. To enterprises of this type belongs the future.

The next lever of industrial progress is the standardization of products, not only such as matches, bricks, fabrics, but the most intricate of machinery. We must ignore the arbitrary wishes of the customer when they arise not from his needs, but from his helplessness. Every customer is forced to improvise and to search instead of being able to find ready-made types best adapted to his needs, and scientifically tested. Standardization must lead to a minimum of types of each product, conforming to the fundamental conditions of the different areas or to the specific nature of the productive requirements.

Standardization is socialization carried into the technical side of production. We see how in this direction technical science in the leading capitalist countries is tearing through the cover of private property, and embarking on what is, in essence, a negation of the principle of competition, 'the freedom of labour' and everything connected with it.

The United States have achieved enormous success in the cheapening of production by the means of standardization of type and quality, and the working out of scientific technical norms of production. 'The Division of Simplified Practice' in conjunction with industrialists and consumers interested in the matter, has done much work covering many dozens of manufactured articles, both large and small. As a result, they have evolved 500 different makes of files, instead of 2,300, 70 makes of barbed wire, instead of 650, 3 types of bricks, instead of 119, 76 types of drill-ploughs, instead of almost 800, and lastly, 45 types of pen-knives, instead of 300. Standardization greets the newly-born; a simplified make of perambulator has resulted in a saving of 1,700 tons of iron and 35 tons of tin. Standardization does not even leave out the sick; the types of hospital beds have been reduced from 40 to one. Burial appurtenances, too, have been standardized; the use of copper, latten, bronze, wool and silk are excluded from the make of a coffin. Economizing on the dead, by means of standardization, saves thousands of tons of metal and coal, hundreds of thousands of metres of timber, etc.

Technical science has compelled recourse to standardization, despite the conditions of capitalism. Socialism imperatively demands standardization, providing as it does, immeasurably greater possibilities for it. But we have, as yet, hardly begun to approach it. The growth of industry has now created the necessary material conditions for the introduction of standardization. All the processes for the renewal of basic capital must proceed along the line of standardization. As compared to the American, the number of types of our products must be reduced to a lower figure.

Standardization not only makes possible but necessitates greater specialization of factories. From the factories where everything is made indifferently, we must evolve factories where some thing is made well.

It must be said to our shame, however, that even to this day, on the eve of the eighth anniversary of our socialist management, we frequently hear the complaint expressed on the part of our industrialists, even engineers, that specialization of production kills 'the spirit', narrows the scope of creative work, makes the work of the factory monotonous, 'dull', and so forth. These snivelling and utterly reactionary objections strongly bring to mind the old Tolstoyan and Populist sermons regarding the superiority of peasant home industries over manufactures. The problem of converting the whole of production into a single, automatically working mechanism is one of the greatest problems that one can imagine. It opens up an enormous field for technical, organizing and economic creative work. The problem can be solved, however, only by a bolder and more persistent specialization of factories, a standardization of production and formation of the big specialized works into one great industrial chain.

The present achievements of foreign laboratories, the vastness of foreign power stations, and the success of American factories in regard to specialization are immeasurably greater than our present achievements along this line. But the conditions of our national and property laws are infinitely more favourable for this purpose than the conditions prevailing in capitalist countries. And in this respect our advantages will the more carry the victory the more we advance. In practice, the problem resolves itself into the gauging of all possibilities and the use of all resources. Results will not be slow in coming, and then we shall be able to sum them up.

CHAPTER SIX

Crises and other dangers of
the world market

When we had scarcely any connection with the world market, the
fluctuating conditions of capitalism reacted on us, not so much
directly through the channels of the goods turnover, as politically,
alternately aggravating and ameliorating our relations with the
capitalist world. As a result, we adopted the habit of regarding the
development of our economic conditions as almost quite apart from
the economic process of the capitalist world. Even after the revival of
our market, with its accompanying trade fluctuations, selling crises,
etc., we still regarded these phenomena independently from capitalist
dynamics in the West and in America. And we were right in so far as
our revival took place within the limits of an almost self-sufficient
economic system. However, with the rapid growth of imports and
exports, the position was radically changed. We are becoming a part, a
highly individual but nevertheless component part, of the world
market. This means that its general factors, though changed, are in
one way or another bound to influence our economic conditions. The
alternating stages of economic conditions are mostly expressed in the
way in which the market buys and sells. We appear on the world
market as sellers and as buyers. Consequently, to some degree, we are
subject to the commercial and industrial flux and reflux of the world
market.

We shall more clearly understand what this means for us if, by
means of comparison, we find out what new element it has brought us.
With every great economic impact (the 'scissors' period, the 'selling'
crisis, and so on), our public opinion became concerned with the
question as to whether crises are inevitable and to what extent, etc. At
the same time, conforming to our economic conditions, we did not

51

step out of the limits of our almost 'self-sufficient' system. We compared the planning principle — the economic basis of which is nationalized industry — with the elemental market principle — the economic basis of which is the peasantry. A combination of planned and elemental economy presents the more difficulties, in that the economic element depends so much on the natural elements. Hence, we arrived at the following prospect: the development of the planning principle will proceed according to the growth of industry and its increasing influence on agriculture and on industrialized methods of cultivation on a co-operative basis, etc. This process, whatever we thought of the degrees of its development, appeared to us an ascending one. But the ascent is in zigzags, and we have just come to a bend in it. This is best seen in the export of our grain.

The problem now is not only the crops, but the sale of crops and that not only on the home but on European markets. The export of grain to Europe depends on the purchasing power of Europe, and the purchasing power of industrial countries (of course, grain is imported by industrial countries) depends on prevailing conditions. In a period of commercial and industrial depression Europe will import less of our grain, still less of our timber, flax, furs, oil and so on, than during a period of industrial prosperity. A decrease in exports is inevitably followed by a decrease in imports. If we do not export a sufficient quantity of raw material and foodstuffs, we are unable to import the necessary quantity of machinery, cotton and so forth. If, as a result of not having disposed of the whole of our export supplies, the purchasing power of the peasant were less than was anticipated, this would lead to a crisis of over-production; on the other hand, should there be a deficiency of goods, we would be unable, owing to curtailed exports, to make good the deficiency by an import of ready-made articles, corresponding machinery, and raw materials, such for instance, as cotton. In other words, a commercial and industrial depression in Europe and more so a world depression, might produce a wave of depression in our own country. And *vice versa,* a commercial and industrial boom in Europe would immediately be followed by a demand for the essential raw materials for industrial purposes such as timber, flax, and also for grain, of which there would be a greater consumption, with the greater prosperity of European populations. Thus, a trade and industrial boom by facilitating the disposal of our export goods, would inevitably provide an impetus to our own commercial, and industrial and agricultural prosperity. Our previous independence of the fluctuations of the world market is going. All the fundamental processes of our economy not only come into close relation with the corresponding processes of the world market, but are being subjected to the laws governing capitalist development, including changing conditions. We thus arrive at a position where, as a business state, it is to our interest, to some extent, at least, to have improved conditions in capitalist countries, for in the other event, if conditions in those countries were to grow worse, it would, to some extent, be to our disadvantage.

This circumstance, rather surprising at a first glance, only reveals on a larger scale the same inconsistencies which are inherent in our so-called New Economic Policy, inconsistencies we used to observe before in the narrower limits of our national 'self-sufficient' economy. Our present order is based not only on the struggle between socialism and capitalism, but — to a certain extent — on the collaboration between them. For the sake of the development of our productive forces, we not only tolerate private capitalist enterprise, but — again to a certain extent— we foster and even 'implant' it by the granting of concessions, and the leasing of works and factories. We are extremely concerned with the development of peasant agriculture, notwithstanding the fact that at the moment it is almost entirely individualistic in character, and that its growth feeds both socialist and capitalist tendencies of development. The danger of the co-existence and collaboration of the two economic systems — the capitalist and the socialist (the latter adopting the methods of the first) — lies in the fact that the capitalist forces may get the best of us.

There was a similar danger within the limits of our 'self-sufficient'* economy, only on a smaller scale. The importance of the control figures of the State Planning Commission, as we have shown in the first chapter, lies in the fact that they have indicated with certainty the predominance of socialist tendencies over the capitalist in the development of the productive forces. If we had intended (or, more truly, if we had been in a position) to remain to the last economically a 'self-sufficient' country, the problem, in essence might have been considered as solved. The only dangers that would then have threatened us would have been political, or a military break through our 'self-sufficient' system from without. But in so far as we have economically entered the system of the world division of labour and

---

* Of course, our economy has never been altogether 'self-sufficient'; it is but for convenience sake that we oppose against each other two clear and definite types.

have thereby become subject to the laws governing the world market, the collaboration and struggle between capitalist and socialist economic tendencies assume immeasurably wider proportions, which mark increased opportunities, but also increased difficulties.

There is, consequently, a profound and quite natural analogy between the problems which used to confront us in the limits of our home economic relations with the institution of the New Economic Policy and the problems which confront us now, as a result of our entry into the world market. The analogy, however, is not complete. The collaboration and struggle between capitalist and socialist tendencies within the Union is proceeding under the vigilant eye of a proletarian State. If in economic questions the Government is not all-powerful, at least the economic forces of the State when the latter consciously fosters the progressive tendency of historic development, become enormous. While tolerating the existence of capitalist tendencies, the workers' State is to some extent able to hold them in check by fostering and encouraging socialist tendencies in every possible way. The means of doing this are: a sound fiscal system and measures of general administration; a system of home and foreign trade; state aid to co-operation; a concessionary policy in strict conformance to national economic needs — in a word, an all-round system of *socialist protection*. These measures presume a dictatorship of the proletariat and their force is consequently limited to the territory of the dictatorship. In the countries with which we have entered into trade relations, an opposite system is in force, that of capitalist protection, in the broadest sense of the word. This is where the difference lies. On Soviet territory, the socialist economy is struggling with the capitalist economy, the former supported by the workers' State. On the territory of the world market, socialism is opposed to capitalism, which in its turn is protected by imperialist States.

Here we have not only economy pitted against economy, but politics against politics. The most effective economic weapons of the workers' state are a monopoly of foreign trade and a policy of concessions. If the laws and methods of the socialist state cannot be imposed on the world market, the relation between the former and the latter will depend largely on the will of the workers' state. Hence a properly regulated system of foreign trade, as we have already shown, assumes a special significance and the importance of a concessionary policy will grow side by side with it.

We do not intend to exhaust this question in the present essay; our purpose has merely been to raise it. The question itself, however, may be divided into two. In the first place, by what means and to what extent can the planned activity of the workers' state safeguard our economy from subjection to the fluctuating conditions of the world market? In the second place, by what means and to what extent can the workers' state safeguard the further development of socialist tendencies in our economy from the capitalist pressure of the world market? We were confronted by both questions in the limits of our 'self-sufficient' economy. They assume new importance and meaning on the broader scale of the world market. In either case the planning principle in economics now assumes much more importance than in the period that has passed. We should inevitably have been subjected by the market had we measured ourselves by the market alone, for the world market is stronger than we are. It would have weakened us by its fluctuating conditions and, having weakened us, would have defeated us by the superior quantity and quality of its goods.

We know that an ordinary capitalist trust endeavours to guard itself against sharp fluctuations of demand and supply. Even a trust closely approximating to the monopoly position never intends to cover the whole of the market with its produce at each given moment. During periods of boom, trusts often allow non-trust enterprises to exist alongside with them, allowing them to cover the surplus demand, thus sparing themselves the risk of a new capital investment. When a new depression comes, the non-trust enterprises are the first to suffer, and they frequently pass into the hands of the trust for a mere song. When another boom comes, the trust is prepared to meet it with increased forces of production. If the demand is again greater than the supply, the trust plays the same game over again. In other words, a capitalist trust endeavours to cover the definite demand only and expands according to the growth of the latter, as far as possible transferring the risk connected with fluctuating conditions to the weaker and casual enterprises, which form, as it were, a productive reserve. Of course, this system is not in force everywhere and always, but it is typical, and serves to explain our meaning. Socialist industry is a trust of trusts. This huge productive combine is still less able to follow all the curves of the market demand than a capitalist trust. A state industrial trust must endeavour to cover the demand guaranteed by all former development, utilising as far as possible the private capitalist reserve for covering the temporary surplus demand that may be followed by a new period of depression. The function of such a

reserve is fulfilled by private industry, including concessionary enterprises, and the volume of goods of the world market. This is what we
meant when we spoke of the importance of regulating our foreign
trade system and our concessionary policy.

The State imports such means of production, such raw materials
and commodities for consumption as are required for the support,
improvement and systematic development of the productive process.
The complex relation, if simplified to a schematic outline, would
present itself thus: during periods of world commercial and industrial
prosperity, our export will increase to some additional extent and will
cause an increase in the purchasing power of the population. It is quite
clear that if our industries were immediately to expend their financial
resources on the import of machinery and material for the expansion
of corresponding branches of production, the next world crisis which
would decrease our economic resources, would also doom us to a crisis
in the over-developed branches of industry and to a certain extent in
all our industries.

Of course, to some extent, such occurrences are inevitable. Peasant
agriculture on the one hand, the world market on the other, these are
the two sources of fluctuation and crises. But the art of economic
policy, however, will consist in covering the growing home demand
by the secure part of state production and the temporary surplus
demand by a temporary import of ready-made goods and the attraction of private capital. Under these circumstances, the alternate
depressions in world conditions would have little influence on our
national industries.

As in the whole of this work the regulation of peasant agriculture
enters as an important, sometimes as a determining element. It shows
how necessary, if we maintain the split-up conditions of our peasant
agriculture, become such organizations as the co-operatives, the
adaptable trading bodies of the State, which must all allow for a much
better and completer calculation and estimation of possible fluctuations in peasant demand and supply.

*   *   *

But does not the process of our 'growth' into the world market
threaten us with greater dangers? In the event of a war or a blockade,
are we not threatened with an automatic break in the innumerable
threads of life? We must not forget that the capitalist world is absolutely hostile to us, etc., etc. Such thoughts seethe in many heads.

Among our industrialists we may find many conscious or semi-conscious supporters of the 'self-sufficient' economy principle. We must devote a few words to this. Of course, loans, concessions, and the growing dependence on exports and imports have their dangers. In no one of these directions can we let go the reins. But there is an opposite danger, equally great; this consists in a slower rate of progress than would be possible by an active utilization of all world possibilities. And we are not free to choose the rate of our development, as we live and grow under the pressure of the world market.

The argument concerning the danger of war or blockade in the event of our 'growth into the world market' is too thread-bare and abstract. In so far as international exchange, in all its forms, makes us economically stronger, it will also strengthen our position in the event of blockade or war. That our enemies may again try to subject us to this experience we do not for a moment doubt. But, in the first place, the more multiform our international relations, the more difficult it will be even for our possible enemies to break them. And, in the second place, even if these eventualities were to come about, we should still be much stronger than we would have been under a 'self-sufficient', and consequently belated, development. In this respect, we may learn something from the historic experience of bourgeois countries. At the end of the nineteenth century and the beginning of the present, Germany developed a powerful industrial system, on the strength of which she became the most active force in world economics. Her foreign trade turnover and her relations with foreign markets, including the overseas, developed enormously in a short space of time. The war put an end to it all. Owing to her geographic position, Germany from the first day of the war was subjected to an almost complete economic blockade. Nevertheless, the whole world was witness to the astounding vitality and endurance of this highly industrialized country. Her former struggle for markets developed an exceptional adaptability of productive apparatus, which she utilized to the full on a limited national scale during the period of the war.

The world division of labour is not a factor we can leave out of account. We can speed up our own development only by an intelligent use of the resources emanating from the existence of the world division of labour.

CHAPTER SEVEN

Concluding remarks

In the whole of my essay I have confined myself exclusively to the economic process and to its logical development, so to speak. Thus, I have consciously excluded from the field of vision all other factors not only influencing economic development but capable of diverting it in another direction. Such a one-sided economic approach is methodologically correct and inevitable when the matter is one of a prospective estimate of a complex process embracing many years. A practical solution of the moment must be adopted every time with a possible calculation of all the factors in their aspects of the moment. But when the matter is one of the prospects of economic development for a whole period ahead we must inevitably divert our attention from 'superstructure' that is to say, from the factor of politics, first of all. A war, for instance, might have a determining influence on our development in one direction, a successful European revolution in another. And this applies not merely to external events. The internal economic process works out its own complex political course, which in its turn, may become a factor of the greatest importance. The economic disintegration of the rural districts into different elements, which, as we have shown does not threaten us with any direct *economic* dangers, that is to say, with a rapid growth of capitalist tendencies at the expense of socialism, may nevertheless, under certain circumstances, generate political tendencies hostile to socialist development.

The political conditions, internal and international, present a complex combination of questions each demanding a separate analysis but closely connected with economics. This analysis does not enter into the subject of our investigation. To point out the fundamental tendencies in the development of the economic foundations does not mean, however, providing a ready-made key to all the changes of the political superstructure, which also possesses its own inner truth, its problems, its difficulties. An orientation of economic prospects does not preclude a political orientation; it makes the latter easier.

Thus, in the process of our analysis, we have purposely put aside the question as to how long the capitalist order will last. How will it change, and in what direction will it develop? Here several variations are admissible. We are not prepared in these concluding lines to investigate them. It is sufficient for us only to name them. Perhaps we may have to return to them in some other connection.

The question of the success of socialism may be settled at its simplest by presuming that there is going to be a proletarian revolution in Europe in the next few years. This 'variation' is by no means the least probable. From the view of socialist prognosis this settles the question. It is clear that given a combination of the economy of the Soviet Union with the economy of Soviet Europe, the question of the comparative coefficients of socialist and capitalist production would be successfully solved, despite any kind of resistance on the part of America. And it is open to doubt that such resistance would last long.

The question becomes more complicated if we hypothetically assume that the capitalist system surrounding us will still continue for several decades. Such an assumption however would be senseless in itself, were it not made more real by other assumptions. In the event of this variation what would become of the European proletariat and then of the American? What would become of the productive forces of capitalism? If the decades hypothetically admitted were to be decades of flux and reflux, cruel civil war, of economic deadlock, and even utter economic collapse, that is to say, were the birth of socialism to be a painful protracted process, it is clear that in the transitional period our economy would acquire superior weight, owing to the incomparably greater stability of our socialized foundations.

If we were to assume however, that in the course of the next decade, a new economic equilibrium would be established on the world market, such, for instance, as prevailed in the period of 1871-1914, the whole question would present a different aspect. A condition for an equilibrium of this kind would have to be a new growth in the productive forces, for the comparative 'peaceful disposition' of the bourgeoisie and the proletariat and the opportunist transformation of social democracy and the trade unions in the decade preceding the war were only due to the tremendous growth of industry. It is quite evident that if the impossible were to become possible, if the improbable became probable, if world capitalism, headed by European capitalism, discovered a new dynamic equilibrium, not only for its unstable government combinations but for its productive forces, if capitalist production were in the next few years and decades to commence another period of mighty growth, this would mean that we, a socialist state, though preparing to change and already changing from a slow goods train to a faster passenger, would still have to catch up the express. To put it more simply, it would mean that we had made a mistake in the fundamental estimation of history. It would mean that capitalism had not yet exhausted its 'missions' in history and that the present imperialist phase was not one of the decline of capitalism, its last convulsions, but the dawn of a new prosperity for it. It is quite clear that under conditions of a new and protracted period of revival of capitalism, both in Europe and the rest of the world, socialism in a backward country would be confronted with great dangers. Of what kind? A new war, which again would not be prevented by a 'duped' European proletariat — a war in which the enemy would oppose us with a superiority of technical resources? Or would it be by an influx of capitalist goods, incomparably better and cheaper than ours, goods which would break our foreign trade monopoly and afterwards the other foundations of our socialist economy? At bottom, this is now a question of secondary importance. It is however, quite clear to Marxists that socialism in a backward country would be very hard pressed if capitalism had the opportunity not only to germinate, but to embark on a long period of development of its productive forces in advanced countries.

However, there are no reasonable grounds to presume a variation of this kind, and it would be senseless first to develop a fantastically optimistic future for the capitalist world and then to break our heads trying to find a way out of it. The European and world system of economy, at the present moment, present such a mass of disparities not conducive to development, but undermining it at every step, that history in the coming years will provide us with sufficient occasion to win the economic race if we properly utilize all the resources of our own and the world's economy. And we are determined to do this. By that time, European development will also have advanced the 'coefficient' of political force on the side of the revolutionary proletariat, despite delays and setbacks. On the whole, the balance of history will, we may presume, come out more than favourably for us.

Problems of Development
of the USSR

1931

Problems of Development
of the USSR

1. Economic contradictions of the transitional period

The contradictory processes in the economy and politics of the USSR are developing on the basis of the dictatorship of the proletariat. The character of the social regime is determined first of all by the property relations. The nationalization of land, of the means of industrial production and exchange, with the monopoly of foreign trade in the hands of the state, constitute the bases of the social order in the USSR. The classes expropriated by the October Revolution, as well as the elements of the bourgeoisie and the bourgeois section of the bureaucracy being newly formed, could re-establish private ownership of land, banks, factories, mills, railroads, etc., only by means of a counter-revolutionary overthrow. These property relations, lying at the base of class relations, determine for us the nature of the Soviet Union as a proletarian state.

The defence of the USSR from foreign intervention and from attack by internal enemies — from the monarchists and former landowners to the 'democrats', the Mensheviks and Socialist Revolutionaries — is the elementary and indisputable duty of every revolutionary worker, all the more so of the Bolshevik-Leninists. Ambiguity and reservations on this question, which in essence reflect the waverings of petty-bourgeois ultra-leftism between the world of imperialism and the world of the proletarian revolution, are incompatible with adherence to the International Left Opposition.

The possibility of the present truly gigantic successes of the Soviet economy was created by the revolutionary overturn of the property relations which established the pre-conditions for a planned elimination of market anarchy. Capitalism never gave and is incapable of giving that progression of economic growth which is developing at present on the territory of the Soviet Union. The unprecedentedly high tempos of industrialization, which have unfolded in spite of the expectations and plans of the epigone leadership, have proved once and for all the might of the socialist method of economy. The frantic struggle of the imperialists against so-called Soviet 'dumping' is an involuntary but for that an all the more genuine recognition on their part of the superiority of the Soviet form of production. In the field of agriculture, where backwardness, isolation and barbarism have their deepest roots, the regime of the proletarian dictatorship also succeeded in revealing a mighty creative power. No matter how great future setbacks and retreats may be, the present tempos of collectivization, possible only on the basis of the nationalization of the land, credit and industry, with the workers in the leading role, signify a new epoch in the development of humanity, the beginning of the liquidation of 'the idiocy of rural life'.

Even in the worst case historically conceivable, if blockade, intervention, or internal civil war should overthrow the proletarian dictatorship, the great lesson of socialist construction would retain all its force for the further development of humanity. The temporarily vanquished October Revolution would be fully justified economically and culturally, and consequently would be reborn. The most important task of the proletarian vanguard, however, is to bar the doors to this worst historical variant, by defending and strengthening the October Revolution and by transforming it into a prologue to the world revolution.

Absolutely false is the official doctrine of fatalistic optimism prevailing today, according to which the continued speedy growth of industrialization and collectivization is assured in advance and leads automatically to the construction of socialism in a single country.

If a highly developed socialist economy is possible only as a harmonious, internally proportionate and consequently crisis-free economy, then on the contrary the transitional economy from capitalism to socialism is a crucible of contradictions where moreover, the deeper and sharper ones lie ahead. The Soviet Union has not entered into socialism, as the ruling Stalinist faction teaches, but only into the first stage of the development in the direction of socialism.

At the core of the economic difficulties, the successive crises, the extreme tension of the whole Soviet system and its political convulsions, lie a number of contradictions of diverse historical origin which are interlinked in various ways. Let us name the most important ones: (a) the heritage of the capitalist and pre-capitalist contradictions of old tsarist-bourgeois Russia, primarily the contradiction between town and country; (b) the contradiction between the general cultural-economic backwardness of Russia and the tasks of socialist transformation which dialectically grow out of it; (c) the contradiction between the workers' state and the capitalist encirclement, particularly between the monopoly of foreign trade and the world market.

These contradictions are not at all of a brief and episodic character; on the contrary, the significance of the most important of them will increase in the future.

The realization of the five-year plan would represent a gigantic step forward compared to the impoverished inheritance which the proletariat snatched from the hands of the exploiters. But even after achieving its first victory in planning, the Soviet Union will not yet have issued out of the first stage of the transition period. Socialism as a system of production not for the market but for the satisfying of human needs is conceivable only on the basis of highly developed productive forces. However, according to the average per capita amount of goods, the USSR even at the end of the five-year plan will still remain one of the most backward countries. In order really to catch up with the advanced capitalist countries, a number of five-year plan programmes will be needed. Meanwhile the industrial successes of recent years in themselves do not at all assure an uninterrupted growth in the future. Precisely the speed of industrial development accumulates disproportions, partly inherited from the past, partly growing out of the complications of the new tasks, partly created by the methodological mistakes of the leadership in combination with direct sabotage. The substitution of economic direction by administrative goading, with the absence of any serious collective verification, leads inevitably to the inclusion of the mistakes in the very foundation of the economy and to the preparation of new 'tight places' inside the economic process. The disproportions driven inward inevitably return at the following stage in the form of disharmony between the means of production and raw materials, between transport and industry, between quantity and quality, and finally in the disorganization of the monetary system. These crises conceal within themselves all the greater dangers the less the present state leadership is capable of foreseeing them in time.

'Complete' collectivization, even were it actually to be carried out in the coming two or three years, would not at all signify the liquidation of the kulaks as a class. The form of producers' co-operatives, given the lack of a technical and cultural base, is incapable of stopping the differentiation within the small commodity producers and the emergence from their midst of capitalist elements. Genuine liquidation of the kulak requires a complete revolution in agricultural technique and the transformation of the peasantry, alongside of the industrial proletariat, into workers of the socialist economy and members if the classless society. But this is a perspective of decades. With the predominance of individual peasant implements and the personal or group interest of their owners, the differentiation of the peasantry will inevitably be renewed and strengthened precisely in the event of a comparatively successful collectivization, that is, with the general increase in agricultural production. If we should further assume that collectivization, together with the elements of new technique, will considerably increase the productivity of agricultural labour, without which collectivization would not be economically justified and consequently would not maintain itself, this would immediately create in the village, which is even now over-populated, ten, twenty, or more millions of surplus workers whom industry would not be able to absorb even with the most optimistic plans. Corresponding to the growth of surplus, that is, of semi-proletarian, semi-pauperized population unable to find a place in the collectives would be the growth at the other pole of rich collectives and more wealthy peasants inside the poor and medium collectives. With a short-sighted leadership, declaring *a priori* that the collectives are socialist enterprises, capitalist-farmer elements can find in collectivization the best cover for themselves, only to become all the more dangerous for the proletarian dictatorship.

The economic successes of the present transition period do not, consequently, liquidate the basic contradictions but prepare their deepened reproduction on a new, higher historical foundation.

Capitalist Russia, in spite of its backwardness, already constituted an inseparable part of the world economy. This dependence of the part upon the whole was inherited by the Soviet republic from the past, together with the whole geographic, demographic and economic structure of the country. The theory of a self-sufficient national socialism, formulated in 1924-27, reflected the first, extremely low period of a revival of the economy after the war, when its world requirements had not yet made themselves felt. The present tense struggle for the extension of Soviet exports is a very vivid refutation of the illusions of national socialism. The foreign-trade figures increasingly become the dominating figures in relation to the plans and tempos of socialist construction. But foreign trade must be continued; and the problem of the mutual relation between the transitional Soviet economy and the world market is just beginning to reveal its decisive significance.

Academically, it is understood, one can construct within the boundaries of the USSR an enclosed and internally balanced socialist economy; but the long historic road to this 'national' ideal would lead through gigantic economic shifts, social convulsions and crises. The mere doubling of the present crop, that is, its approach to the European, would confront the Soviet economy with the huge task of realizing an agricultural surplus of tens of millions of tons. A solution to this problem, as well as to the no less acute problem of growing rural over-population, could be achieved only by a radical redistribution of millions of people among the various branches of the economy and by the complete liquidation of the contradictions between the city and the village. But this task — one of the basic tasks of socialism — would in turn require the utilization of the resources of the world market in a measure hitherto unknown.

In the last analysis, all the contradictions of the development of the USSR lead in this manner to the contradictions between the isolated workers' state and its capitalist encirclement. The impossibility of constructing a self-sufficient socialist economy in a single country revives the basic contradictions of socialist construction at every new stage on an extended scale and in greater depth. In this sense, the dictatorship of the proletariat in the USSR would inevitably have to suffer destruction if the capitalist regime in the rest of the world should prove to be capable of maintaining itself for another long historical epoch. However, to consider such a perspective as the inevitable or even the most probable one can be done only by those who believe in the firmness of capitalism or its longevity. The Left Opposition has nothing in common with such capitalist optimism. But it can just as little agree with the theory of national socialism which is an expression of capitulation before capitalist optimism.

The problem of foreign trade in its present exceptional acuteness caught the leading bodies of the USSR unawares, and by that alone became an element of disruption of the economic plans. In the face of this problem, the leadership of the Comintern also proved to be bankrupt. World unemployment made the question of developing the economic relations between the capitalist countries and the USSR a vital problem for broad masses of the working class. Before the Soviet government and the Comintern there opened up a rare opportunity to attract the social democratic and non-party workers on the basis of a vital and burning question and so to acquaint them with the Soviet five-year plan and with the advantages of the socialist methods of economy. Under the slogan of economic collaboration and armed with a concrete programme, the communist vanguard could have led a far more genuine struggle against the blockade and intervention than through repetition of one-and-the-same bare condemnations. The perspective of a planned European and world economy could have been raised to unprecedented heights and in this manner could have given new nourishment to the slogans of the world revolution. The Comintern did almost nothing in this field.

When the world bourgeois press, including the social-democratic press, was suddenly mobilized for a campaign of incitement against alleged Soviet dumping, the Communist parties marked time at a loss for what to do. At a time when the Soviet government, before the eyes of the whole world, seeks foreign markets and credits, the bureaucracy of the Comintern declares the slogan of economic collaboration with the USSR a 'counter-revolutionary' slogan. Such shameful stupidities, as if especially created for confusing the working class, are a direct consequence of the ruinous theory of socialism in one country.

2. The party in the regime of the dictatorship

The *economic* contradictions of the transitional economy do not develop in a vacuum. The *political* contradictions of the regime of the dictatorship, even though in the final analysis they grow out of the economic, have an independent and also a more direct significance for the fate of the dictatorship than the economic crisis.

The present official teaching, according to which the growth of nationalized industry and collectives automatically and uninterruptedly strengthens the regime of the proletarian dictatorship, is a product of vulgar 'economic' and not dialectical materialism. In reality, the inter-relationship between the economic foundation and the political superstructure has a far more complex and contradictory character, particularly in the revolutionary epoch. The dictatorship of the proletariat, which grew out of bourgeois social relations, revealed its might in the period preceding the nationalization of industry and collectivization of agriculture. Later on, the dictatorship passed through periods of strengthening and weakening, depending upon the course of the internal and world class struggle. Economic achievements were often bought at the price of politically weakening the regime. Precisely this dialectical inter-relationship between economy and politics directly produced sharp turns in the economic policy of the government, beginning with the New Economic Policy and ending with the latest zigzags in collectivization.

Like all political institutions, the party is in the last instance a product of the productive relations of society. But it is not at all an automatic recorder of the changes in these relationships. As the synthesis of the historical experiences of the proletariat, in a certain sense of the whole of humanity, the party rises above the conjunctural and episodic changes in the economic and political conditions, which only invest it with the necessary power of foresight, initiative and resistance.

It can be considered entirely irrefutable that the dictatorship was achieved in Russia and afterwards withstood the most critical moments because it had its centre of consciousness and determination in the form of the Bolshevik Party. The inconsistency and, in the final analysis, the reactionary nature of all species of anarchists and anarcho-syndicalists consists precisely in the fact that they do not understand the decisive significance of the revolutionary party, particularly at the highest stage of the class struggle, in the epoch of the proletarian dictatorship. Without a doubt, social contradictions can reach such an acute point that no party can find a way out. But it is no less true that with the weakening of the party or with its degeneration even an avoidable crisis in the economy can become the cause for the fall of the dictatorship.

The economic and political contradictions of the Soviet regime intersect within the leading party. The acuteness of the danger depends, with each succeeding crisis, directly upon the state of the party. No matter how great the significance of the rate of industrialization and collectivization may be in itself, it nevertheless takes second place before the problem: has the party retained Marxist clarity of vision, ideological solidity, the ability to arrive collectively at an opinion and to fight self-sacrificingly for it? From this point of view, the state of the party is the highest test of the condition of the proletarian dictatorship, a synthesized measure of its stability. If, in the name of achieving this or that practical aim, a false theoretical attitude is foisted on the party; if the party ranks are forcibly ousted from political leadership; if the vanguard is dissolved into the amorphous mass; if the party cadres are kept in obedience by the apparatus of state repression — then it means that in spite of the economic successes, the general balance of the dictatorship shows a deficit.

Only blind people, hirelings, or the deceived can deny the fact that the ruling party of the USSR, the leading party of the Comintern, has been completely crushed and replaced by the apparatus. The gigantic difference between the bureaucratism of 1923 and the bureaucratism of 1931 is determined by the complete liquidation of the dependence of the apparatus upon the party that took place in this span of years, as well as by the plebiscitary degeneration of the apparatus itself.

Not a trace remains of party democracy. Local organizations are selected and autocratically reorganized by secretaries. New members of the party are recruited according to orders from the centre with the methods of compulsory political service. The local secretaries are appointed by the Central Committee, which is officially and openly converted into a consultative body of the general secretary. Congresses are arbitrarily postponed, delegates are selected from the top according to their demonstration of solidarity with the irreplaceable leader. Even a pretence of control over the top by the lower ranks is removed. The members of the party are systematically trained in the spirit of passive subordination. Every spark of independence, self-reliance and firmness, that is, those features which make up the nature of a revolutionist, is crushed, hounded and trampled underfoot.

In the apparatus there undoubtedly remain not a few honest and devoted revolutionists. But the history of the post-Lenin period — a chain of ever-grosser falsification of Marxism, of unprincipled manoeuvres and of cynical mockeries of the party — would have been impossible without the growing predominance in the apparatus of servile officials who stop at nothing.

In the guise of spurious monolithism, double-dealing permeates the whole of party life. The official decisions are accepted unanimously. At the same time, all the party strata are corroded by irreconcilable contradictions which seek roundabout ways for their eruption. The Bessedovskys direct the purging of the party against the Left Opposition on the eve of their desertion to the camp of the enemy. The Blumkins are shot down and replaced by Agabekovs. Syrtsov, appointed chairman of the People's Commissars of the RSFSR in place of the 'semi-traitor' Rykov, is very soon accused of underground work against the party. Ryazanov, the head of the most important scientific institution of the party, is accused, after the solemn celebration of his jubilee, of being a participant in a counter-revolutionary plot. In freeing itself of party control, the bureaucracy deprives itself of the possibility of controlling the party except through the GPU, where the Menzhinskys and Yagodas put up the Agabekovs.

A steam boiler, even under rude handling, can do useful work for a long time. A manometer, however, is a delicate instrument which is very quickly ruined under impact. With an unserviceable manometer the best of boilers can be brought to the point of explosion. If the party were only an instrument of orientation, like a manometer or a compass on a ship, even in such a case its derangement would spell great trouble. But more than that, the party is the most important part of the governing mechanism. The Soviet boiler hammered out by the October Revolution is capable of doing gigantic work even with poor mechanics. But the very derangement of the manometer signifies the constant danger of explosion of the whole machine.

The apologists and attorneys for the Stalinist bureaucracy attempt at times to represent the bureaucratic liquidation of the party as a progressive process of the dissolution of the party into the class, which is explained by the successes of the socialist transformation of society. In these theoretical throes, illiteracy competes with charlatanry. One could speak of the dissolution of the party into the class only as the reverse side of the easing of class antagonisms, the dying away of politics, the reduction to zero of all forms of bureaucratism, and primarily the *reduction of the role of coercion* in social relations. However, the processes taking place in the USSR and in the ruling party have a directly opposite character in many respects. Coercive discipline is not only not dying away — it would be ridiculous even to expect this at the present stage — but, on the contrary, it is assuming an exceptionally severe character in all the spheres of social and personal life. Organized participation in the politics of the party and the class is actually reduced to zero. The corruption of bureaucratism knows no limits. Under these conditions, to represent the dictatorship of the Stalinist apparatus as the socialist dying away of the party is a mockery of the dictatorship and of the party.

The right-wing camp followers of centrism, the Brandlerites, try to justify the strangulation of the party by the Stalinist bureaucracy with references to the 'lack of culture' of the working masses. This does not at all prevent them, at the same time, from awarding the Russian proletariat the dubious monopoly in the construction of socialism in one country.

The general economic and cultural backwardness of Russia is unquestionable. But the development of historically retarded nations has a *combined* character: in order to overcome their backwardness, they are compelled in many fields to adopt and to cultivate the most advanced forms. The scientific doctrine of proletarian revolution was created by the revolutionists of backward Germany in the middle of the nineteenth century. Thanks to its retardation, German capitalism later outstripped the capitalism of England and France. The industry of backward bourgeois Russia was the most concentrated in the whole world. The young Russian proletariat was the first to show in action the combination of a general strike and an uprising, the first to create soviets, and the first to conquer power. The backwardness of Russian capitalism did not prevent the education of the most farsighted proletarian party that ever existed. On the contrary, it made it possible.

As the selection of the revolutionary class in a revolutionary epoch, the Bolshevik Party lived a rich and stormy internal life in the most critical period of its history. Who would have dared, prior to October or in the first years after the revolution, to refer to the 'backwardness' of the Russian proletariat as a defence of bureaucratism in the party! However, the genuine rise in the general cultural level of the workers which had occurred since the seizure of power did not lead to the flourishing of party democracy, but, on the contrary, to its complete extinction. The references to the stream of workers from the village explain nothing, for this factor has always been in operation and the cultural level of the village since the revolution has risen considerably. Finally, the party is not the class, but its vanguard; it cannot pay for its numerical growth by the lowering of its political level. The Brandlerite defence of plebiscitary bureaucratism, which is based upon a trade-union and not a Bolshevik conception of the party, is in reality self-defence, because in the period of the worst failures and the degradation of centrism, the right-wingers were its most reliable prop.

To explain as a Marxist why the centrist bureaucracy triumphed and why it was compelled to strangle the party in order to preserve its victory, one must proceed not from an abstract 'lack of culture' of the proletariat, but from the change in the mutual relations of the classes and the change in the moods of each class.

After the heroic straining of forces in the years of revolution and civil war, a period of great hopes and inevitable illusions, the proletariat could not but go through a lengthy period of weariness, decline in energy, and in part direct disillusionment in the results of the revolution. By virtue of the laws of the class struggle, the reaction in the proletariat resulted in a tremendous flow of new hope and confidence in the petty-bourgeois strata of the city and village and in the bourgeois elements of the state bureaucracy who gained considerable strength on the basis of the NEP. The crushing of the Bulgarian uprising in 1923, the inglorious defeat of the German proletariat in 1923 and the crushing of the Estonian insurrection in 1924, the treacherous liquidation of the general strike in England in 1926, the crushing of the Chinese revolution in 1927, the stabilization of capitalism connected with all these catastrophes — such is the international setting of the struggle of the centrists against the Bolshevik-Leninists. The abuse of the 'permanent,' that is, in essence, of the international revolution, the rejection of a bold policy of industrialization and collectivization, the reliance upon the kulak, the alliance with the 'national' bourgeoisie in the colonies and with the social imperialists in the metropolis — such are the political contents of the bloc of the centrist bureaucracy with the forces of Thermidor. Supporting itself on the strengthened and emboldened petty-bourgeois and bourgeois bureaucracy, exploiting the passivity of the weary and disoriented proletariat and the defeats of the revolution the world over, the centrist apparatus crushed the left revolutionary wing of the party in the course of a few years.

The political zigzags of the apparatus are not accidental. In them is expressed the adaptation of the bureaucracy to conflicting class forces. The course of 1923-38, if we leave aside occasional waverings, constituted a semi-capitulation of the bureaucracy to the kulaks at home and the world bourgeoisie and its reformist agency abroad. Having felt the increasing hostility of the proletariat, having seen the bottom of the Thermidorean abyss to whose very edge they had slid, the Stalinists leaped to the left. The abruptness of the leap corresponded to the extent of the panic created in their ranks by the consequences of their own policy, laid bare by the criticism of the Left Opposition. The course of 1928-31 — if we again leave aside the

inevitable waverings and backslidings — represents an attempt of the
bureaucracy to adapt itself to the proletariat, but without abandoning
the principled basis of its policy or, what is most important, its
omnipotence. The zigzags of Stalinism show that the bureaucracy is
not a class, not an independent historical factor, but an instrument, an
executive organ of the classes. The left zigzag is proof that no matter
how far the preceding right course had gone, it nevertheless
developed on the basis of the dictatorship of the proletariat. The
bureaucracy, however, is not a passive organ which only refracts the
inspirations of the class. Without having absolute independence, the
illusion of which lives in the skulls of many bureaucrats, the ruling
apparatus nevertheless enjoys a great relative independence. The
bureaucracy is in direct possession of state power; it raises itself above
the classes and puts a powerful stamp upon their development; and
even if it cannot itself become the foundation of state power, it can
with its policy, greatly facilitate the transfer of power from the hands
of one class into the hands of another.

Standing above all the other problems of the bureaucracy is the
problem of self-preservation. All its turns result *directly* from its
striving to retain its independence, its position, its power. But the
policy of zigzags, which requires a completely free hand, is incompat
ible with the presence of an independent party, which is accustomed
to control and demands an accounting. From this flows the system of
the violent destruction of party ideology and the conscious sowing of
confusion.

The kulak course, the Menshevik-saboteur programme of indus
trialization and collectivization, the bloc with Purcell, Chiang Kai
shek, La Follette, and Radich, the creation of the Peasants' 'Interna
tional', the slogan of a two-class party — all this was declared to be
Leninism. On the contrary, the course of industrialization and collec
tivization, the demand for party democracy, the slogan of soviets i
China, the struggle against the two-class parties on behalf of the part
of the proletariat, the exposure of the emptiness and falsehood of the
Krestintern, the Anti-Imperialist League, and other Potemkin vil
lages — all these were given the name of 'Trotskyism'.

With the turn of 1928, the masks were repainted but the mas
querade continued. The proclamation of an armed uprising an
soviets in China at a time of counter-revolutionary ascent, the adven
turistic economic tempos in the USSR under the administrativ
whip, the 'liquidation of the kulak as a class' within two years, the

rejection of the slogans of revolutionary democracy for historically backward countries, the proclamation of the 'third period' at a time of economic revival — all this was now called Leninism. On the contrary, the demand for realistic economic plans adapted to the resources and needs of the workers, the rejection of the programme of the liquidation of the kulaks on the basis of the peasant inventory, the rejection of the metaphysics of the 'third period' for a Marxist analsysis of the economic and political processes throughout the world and in each country — all this was now declared to be 'counterrevolutionary Trotskyism'.

The ideological connection between the two periods of the bureaucratic masquerade remains the theory of socialism in one country, the basic charter of the Soviet bureaucracy which it holds over the world proletarian vanguard and which it uses to sanctify in advance all its actions, turns, errors and crimes. The fabric of party consciousness is created slowly and requires constant renewal by means of a Marxist evaluation of the road passed, of an analysis of the changes in the situation, of a revolutionary prognosis. Without tireless critical internal work, the party inevitably falls into decline. However, the struggle of the bureaucracy for self-preservation excludes an open contrast of today's policy with that of yesterday, that is, the testing of one zigzag by the other. The heavier the conscience of the ruling faction, the more it is transformed into an order of oracles, who speak an esoteric language and demand an acknowledgment of the infallibility of the chief oracle. The whole history of the party and the revolution is adapted to the needs of bureaucratic self-preservation. One legend is heaped upon another. The basic truths of Marxism are branded as deviations. Thus, in the process of zigzagging between classes for the last eight years, the basic fabric of party consciousness has been ripped apart and torn to pieces more and more. Administrative pogroms did the rest.

Having conquered and strangled the party, the bureaucracy cannot permit itself the luxury of differences of opinion within its own ranks, so as not to be compelled to appeal to the masses to settle the disputed questions. It needs a standing arbitrator, a political superior. The selection for the whole apparatus takes place around the 'chief.' That is how the plebiscitary apparatus regime has come into being.

Bonapartism is one of the forms of the victory of the bourgeoisie over the uprising of the popular masses. To identify the present Soviet regime with the social regime of Bonapartism, as Kautsky does, means consciously to conceal from the workers, in the interests of the bourgeoisie, the difference in class foundations. Notwithstanding this, one can speak with full justification of the complete plebiscitary degeneration of the Stalinist apparatus or of the Bonapartist system of administering the party as one of the preconditions for a Bonapartist regime in the country. A new political order does not arise out of nowhere. The class which has come to power builds the apparatus of its domination from the elements that are at hand at the moment of the revolutionary or the counter-revolutionary overthrow. The Soviets led by the Mensheviks and the Social Revolutionaries were, in Kerensky's day, the last political resource of the bourgeois regime. At the same time, the Soviets, above all in their Bolshevik form, were the crucible of the dictatorship of the proletariat which was in the process of creation. The present-day Soviet apparatus is a bureaucratic, plebiscitary, distorted form of the dictatorship of the proletariat. It is also, however, a potential instrument of Bonapartism. Between the present function of the apparatus and its possible function, the blood of civil war would still have to flow. Yet the victorious counter-revolution would find precisely in the plebiscitary apparatus invaluable elements for the establishment of its domination, just as its very victory would be unthinkable without the transfer of decisive sections of the apparatus to the side of the bourgeoisie. That is why the Stalinist plebiscitary regime has become a main danger for the dictatorship of the proletariat.

3. Dangers and possibilities
of a counter-revolutionary upheaval.

Through the combined effect of economic successes and administrative measures, the specific gravity of the capitalist elements in the economy has been greatly reduced in recent years, especially in industry and trade. The collectivization and the de-kulakization have strongly diminished the exploitive role of the rural upper strata. The relationship of forces between the socialist and the capitalist elements of the economy has undoubtedly been shifted to the benefit of the former. To ignore, or even to deny this fact, as the ultra-lefts or the vulgar oppositionists do, repeating general phrases about Nepmar and Kulak, is entirely unworthy of Marxists.

It is no less false, however, to regard the present percentual rela tionship of forces as assured or, what is worse yet, to measure the degree of the realization of socialism by the specific gravity of state and private economy in the USSR. The accelerated liquidation of the internal capitalist elements, with methods of administrative dizziness here as well, coincided with the accelerated appearance of the USSR on the world market. The question of the specific gravity of the capitalist elements in the USSR, therefore, should not be posed independently of the question of the specific gravity of the USSR in the world economy.

Nepman, middleman, and kulak are undoubtedly natural agents of world imperialism; the weakening of the former signifies at the same time the weakening of the latter. But this does not exhaust the question: besides the Nepman there still exists the state official. Lenin recalled at the last congress in which he participated that not infrequently in history did a victorious people, at least its upper stratum, adopt the customs and mores of the culturally superior people conquered by it, and that analogous processes are also possible in the struggle of classes. The Soviet bureaucracy, which represents an amalgam of the upper stratum of the victorious proletariat with broad strata of the overthrown classes, includes within itself a mighty agency of world capital.

Two trials — against the specialist-saboteurs and against the Mensheviks — have given an extremely striking picture of the relationship of forces of the classes and the parties in the USSR. It was irrefutably established by the court that during the years 1923-28 the bourgeois specialists, in close alliance with the foreign centres of the bourgeoisie, successfully carried through an artificial slowdown of industrialization, counting upon the re-establishment of capitalist relationships. The elements of dual power in the land of the proletarian dictatorship attained such a weight that the direct agents of the capitalist restoration, together with their democratic agents, the Mensheviks, could play a leading role in all the economic centres of the Soviet republic! How far, on the other hand, has centrism slipped down in the direction of the bourgeoisie when the official policy of the party for a number of years could serve as the legal cover for the plans and methods of capitalist restoration!

The left zigzag of Stalin, objective evidence of the powerful vitality of the proletarian dictatorship, which turns the bureaucracy around on its own axis, in any case created neither a consistent proletarian policy nor a full blooded regime of the proletarian dictatorship. The elements of dual power contained in the bureaucratic apparatus have not disappeared with the inauguration of the new course, but have changed their colour and their methods. They have undoubtedly even become stronger as the plebiscitary degeneration of the apparatus has progressed. The wreckers now invest the tempos with an adventurist scope and thereby prepare dangerous crises. The bureaucrats zealously hang the banner of socialism over the collective farms in which the kulaks are hiding. Not only ideological but also organizational tentacles of the counter-revolution have penetrated deeply into the organs of the proletarian dictatorship, assuming a protective colouration all the more easily since the whole life of the official party rests upon lies and falsification. The elements of dual power are all the more dangerous the less the suppressed proletarian vanguard has the possibility of uncovering them and purging its ranks in time.

Politics is concentrated economics, and the politics of the dictatorship the most concentrated of any politics conceivable. The plan of economic perspectives is not a dogma given at the outset, but a working hypothesis. Collective examination of the plan must take place in the process of its execution, in which the elements of verification are not only bookkeeping figures but also the muscles and the nerves of the workers and the political moods of the peasants. To test, to check up, to summarize, and to generalize all this can only be done by an independent party, acting of its own free will, sure of itself. The five-year plan would be inconceivable without the certainty that all the participants in the economic process, the managements of the factories and trusts on the one hand and the factory committees on the other, submit to party discipline, and that the nonparty workers remain under the leadership of the central units and the factory committees.

Party discipline, however, is completely fused with administrative discipline. The apparatus showed itself — and still shows itself even today — as all-powerful, insofar as it has the possibility of expending the basic capital of the Bolshevik Party. The capital is large, but not unlimited. The overstraining of bureaucratic command reached its highest limits at the moment of the crushing of the right wing. One can go no further on this road. But this has prepared the way for the collapse of administrative discipline.

From the moment when party tradition for some and fear of it for others ceases to hold the official party together, and hostile forces break through to the surface, the state economy will suddenly feel the full force of the political contradictions. Every trust and every factory will cancel the plans and directives coming from above, in order to insure their interests by their own means. Contracts between single factories and the private market, behind the back of the state, will become the rule instead of the exception. The struggle between the factories for workers, raw materials, and markets will automatically impel the workers to struggle for better working conditions. The planning principle, inescapably abrogated in this manner, would not only signify the re-establishment of the internal market but also the disruption of the monopoly of foreign trade. The managements of the trusts would quickly approach the position of private owners or agents of foreign capital, to which many of them would be compelled to turn in their struggle for existence. In the village, where the types of collective farms which are not very capable of offering resistance would hardly have time to absorb the small commodity producers, the collapse of the planning principle would precipitously unleash elements of primitive accumulation. Administrative pressure would be unable to save the situation if only for the fact that the bureaucratic apparatus would be the first victim of the contradictions and centrifugal tendencies. Without the idealistic and cementing force of the Communist Party, the Soviet state and the planned economy would consequently be condemned to disintegration.

The collapse of plebiscitary discipline would not only embrace the party, administrative, economic, trade-union, and cooperative organs, but also the Red Army and the GPU; under certain conditions, the explosion might begin with the latter. This already shows that the passage of power into the hands of the bourgeoisie could in no case be confined simply to a process of degeneration alone, but would inevitably have to assume the form of an open violent overthrow.

In what political form could this take place? In this respect, only the main tendencies can be revealed. By *Thermidorean* overthrow, the Left Opposition always understood a decisive shift of power from the proletariat to the bourgeoisie, but accomplished formally within the framework of the Soviet system under the banner of one faction of the official party against the other. In contrast to this, the *Bonapartist* overthrow appears as a more open, 'riper' form of the bourgeois counter-revolution, carried out against the Soviet system and the Bolshevik Party as a whole, in the form of the naked sword raised in the name of bourgeois property. The crushing of the right wing of the party and its renunciation of its platform diminish the chances of the

first, step-by-step, veiled, that is Thermidorean form of the overthrow. The plebiscitary degeneration of the party apparatus undoubtedly increases the chances of the Bonapartist form. However, Thermidor and Bonapartism represent no irreconcilable class types, but
are only stages of development of the same type — the living historic
process is inexhaustible in the creation of transitional and combined
forms. One thing is sure: were the bourgeoisie to dare to pose the
question of power openly, the final answer would be given in the
mutual testing of class forces in mortal combat.

In the event that the molecular process of the accumulation of
contradictions were to lead to an explosion, the unification of the
enemy camp would be accomplished under fire around those political
centres which yesterday were still illegal. Centrism, as the commanding faction, together with the administrative apparatus, would
immediately fall victim to political differentiation. The elements of its
composition would divide into opposite sides on the barricades. Who
would occupy the main place at first in the camp of the counter-
revolution: the adventurist-praetorian elements of the type of
Tukhachevsky, Bluecher, Budenny, downright refuse of the type of
Bessedovsky, or still weightier elements of the type of Ramzin and
Osadchy? That will be determined by the time and the conditions of
the turn of the counter-revolution to the offensive. Still the question
itself could only be of episodic significance. The Tukhachevskys and
Bessedovskys could serve only as a step for the Ramzins and Osad-
chys; they, for their part, will only be a step for the imperialist
dictatorship that would very soon fling aside both, should it not
succeed in leaping over them immediately. The Mensheviks and
Social Revolutionaries would form a bloc with the praetorian wing of
centrism and serve to cover for the imperialists on the precipitous
decline of the revolution as they sought to cover for them in 1917
during the revolution's sharp ascent.

In the opposing camp, a no less decisive regrouping of forces would
take place under the banner of the struggle for October. The
revolutionary elements of the Soviets, the trade unions, the coopera-
tives, the army, and, finally and above all, the advanced workers in
the factories would feel, in the face of the threatening danger, the need
to join together closely under clear slogans around the tempered and
tested revolutionary cadre which is incapable of capitulation and
betrayal. Not only the centrist faction but also the right wing of the
party would produce not a few revolutionists who would defend the

October Revolution with arms in hand. But for this they would need a painful internal demarcation, which cannot be carried out without a period of confusion, vacillation, and loss of time. Under these decisive circumstances, the faction of the Bolshevik-Leninists, sharply marked out by its past and steeled by difficult tests, would serve as the element for a crystallization within the party. All around the Left Opposition would take place the process of the unification of the revolutionary camp and the rebirth of the true Communist Party. The presence of a Leninist faction would double the chances of the proletariat in the struggle against the forces of the counter-revolutionary overthrow.

4. The Left Opposition and the USSR

The democratic tasks of backward Russia could be solved only through the road of the dictatorship of the proletariat. Having captured power at the head of the peasant masses, the proletariat could not, however, stop short at the democratic tasks. The democratic revolution was directly interwoven with the first stage of the socialist revolution. But the latter cannot be completed except on the international arena. The programme of the Bolshevik Party formulated by Lenin regards the October upheaval as the first stage of the proletarian world revolution, from which it is inseparable. This is also the kernel of the theory of the *permanent revolution*.

The extraordinary delay in the development of the world revolution, which creates gigantic difficulties for the USSR and produces unexpected transitional processes, nevertheless does not change the fundamental perspectives and tasks which flow from the world-embracing character of capitalist economy and from the permanent character of the proletarian world revolution.

The International Left Opposition rejects and condemns categorically the theory of socialism in one country, created in 1924 by the epigones, as the worst perversion of Marxism, as the principal achievement of Thermidorean ideology. Irreconcilable combat against Stalinism (or national socialism), which has found its expression in the programme of the Communist International is a necessary condition for correct revolutionary strategy, in the questions of the international class struggle as well as in the sphere of the economic tasks of the USSR.

If we proceed from the incontestable fact that the Communist Party of the Soviet Union has ceased to be a party, are we not thereby forced to the conclusion that there is no dictatorship of the proletariat in the USSR, since this is inconceivable without a ruling proletarian party? Such a conclusion, entirely consistent at first sight, is nevertheless a caricature of the reality, a reactionary caricature that ignores the creative possibilities of the regime and the hidden reserves of the dictatorship. Even if the party as a party, that is, as an independent organization of the vanguard, does not exist, this does not yet mean that all the elements of the party inherited from the past are liquidated. In the working class, the tradition of the October overthrow is alive and strong; firmly rooted are the habits of class thought; unforgotten in the older generation are the lessons of the revolutionary struggles and the conclusions of Bolshevik strategy; in the masses of the people and especially in the proletariat lives the hatred against the former ruling classes and their parties. All these tendencies in their entirety constitute not only the reserve of the future, but also the living power of today, which preserves the Soviet Union as a workers' state.

Between the creative forces of the revolution and the bureaucracy there exists a profound antagonism. If the Stalinist apparatus constantly comes to a halt at certain limits, if it finds itself compelled even to turn sharply to the left, this occurs above all under the pressure of the amorphous, scattered, but still powerful elements of the revolutionary party. The strength of this factor cannot be expressed numerically. At any rate, it is today powerful enough to support the structure of the dictatorship of the proletariat. To ignore it means to adopt the bureaucratic manner of thinking and to seek out the party wherever the Stalinist apparatus commands and nowhere else.

The Left Opposition categorically rejects the analysis of the Soviet state not only as a bourgeois or petty-bourgeois state, but also as a 'neutral' state that has remained in some way without class rulers. The presence of *elements* of dual power in no way signifies the *political equilibrium of the classes*. In evaluating social processes, the establishment of the degree of maturity attained and the point of termination is especially important. The moment of change from quantity to quality has a decisive significance in politics as well as in other fields. The correct determination of this moment is one of the most important and at the same time most difficult tasks of the revolutionary leadership.

The evaluation of the USSR as a state standing between the classes

(Urbahns) is theoretically inadequate and politically equivalent to a surrender in whole or in part of the fortress of the world proletariat to the class enemy. The Left Opposition rejects and condemns categorically this standpoint as incompatible with the principles of revolutionary Marxism.

The analysis given above of the possibilities and chances of a counterrevolutionary overthrow should in no sense be understood to mean that the present contradictions must *absolutely* lead to the open explosion of civil war. The social sphere is elastic and — within certain limits — opens up various possibilities, in accordance with the energy and the penetration of the battling forces, with the internal processes dependent upon the course of the international class struggle. The duty of the proletarian revolutionist consists under all circumstances in thinking out every situation to the end and also of being prepared for the worst outcome. The Marxist analysis of the possibilities and chances of a Thermidorean-Bonapartist overthrow has nothing in common with pessimism, just as the blindness and bragging of the bureaucracy has nothing in common with revolutionary optimism.

The recognition of the present Soviet state as a workers' state not only signifies that the bourgeoisie can conquer power only by means of an armed uprising but also that the proletariat of the USSR has not forfeited the possibility of subordinating the bureaucracy to it, of reviving the party again, and of regenerating the regime of the dictatorship — without a new revolution, with the methods and on the road of *reform*.

It would be sterile pedantry to undertake to calculate in advance the chances of proletarian reform and of the attempts at a bourgeois upheaval. It would be criminal lightheartedness to contend that the former is assured, the latter excluded. One must be prepared for all possible variants. In order, at the moment of the inevitable collapse of the plebiscitary regime, to assemble and to push ahead the proletarian wing promptly, without letting the class enemy gain time, it is absolutely necessary that the Left Opposition exist and develop as a firm faction, that it analyse all the changes in the situation, formulate clearly the perspectives of development, raise fighting slogans at the right time, and strengthen its connections with the advanced elements of the working class.

The attitude of the Left Opposition to centrism determines its attitude to the Right Opposition, which only constitutes an uncompleted bridge from centrism to the social democracy.

In the Russian question, as well as in all others, the international right wing leads a parasitic existence, nourishing itself chiefly upon the criticism of the practical and secondary mistakes of the Comintern, whose opportunist policy it approves in fundamental questions. The unprincipledness of the Brandlerites shows itself most nakedly and cynically in the questions which are bound up with the fate of the USSR. In the period of the government's betting on the kulaks the Brandlerites completely supported the official course and demonstrated that no policy other than that of Stalin-Rykov-Bukharin could be carried out. After the turn of 1928, the Brandlerites were reduced to an expectant silence. When the successes of the industrialization, unexpected by them, showed themselves, the Brandlerites uncritically adopted the programme of the 'five-year plan in four years' and the 'liquidation of the kulaks as a class'. The right-wingers demonstrated their complete incapacity for a revolutionary orientation and Marxist foresight, coming forward at the same time as the advocates of the Stalinist regime in the USSR. The characteristic feature of opportunism — to bow before the power of the day — determines the whole attitude of the Brandlerites to the Stalinists: 'We are prepared to acknowledge uncritically everything you do in the USSR, permit us only to carry out *our* policy in *our* Germany.' The position of the Lovestoneites in the United States, of the Right Opposition in Czechoslovakia, and their related semi-social democratic, semi-communist groups in other countries, bears a similar character.

The Left Opposition conducts an irreconcilable struggle against the right-wing camp followers of the centrists, especially and principally on the basis of the Russian question and at the same time endeavours liberate from the disintegrating influence of the Brandlerite leaders those worker-revolutionists who were driven into the Right Opposition by the zig zags of centrism and its worthless regime.

The petty-bourgeois camp followers, the 'friends' of the Soviet Union, in actuality friends of the Stalinist bureaucracy, including also the officials dependent upon the Comintern in the various countries, lightheartedly close their eyes to the contradictions in the development of the Soviet Union, in order later, at the first serious danger, to turn their backs upon it.

Political and personal conflicts, however, not infrequently also push into the ranks of the Left Opposition frightened centrists or, still worse, unsatisfied careerists. With the sharpening of the repressions, or when the official course is having momentary success, these elements return to the official ranks as capitulators, where they constitute the chorus of the pariahs. The capitulators of the Zinoviev-Pyatakov-Radek type are only very little distinguished from the Menshevik capitulators of the type of Groman-Sukhanov, or from the bourgeois specialists of the type of Ramzin. With all the distinctions in their points of departure, all three groups now meet in recognition of the correctness of the present 'general line', only to scatter in different directions at the next accentuation of the contradictions.

The Left Opposition feels itself a component part of the army of the proletarian dictatorship and of the world revolution; it approaches the tasks of the Soviet regime not from without but from within, fearlessly tears down the false masks, and exposes the real dangers, in order to fight against them with self-sacrifice and to teach others to do the same.

The experience of the whole post-Lenin period bears testimony to the incontestable influence of the Left Opposition upon the course of development of the USSR. All that was creative in the official course — and has remained creative — was a belated echo of the ideas and slogans of the Left Opposition. The half breach in the right-centre bloc resulted from the pressure of the Bolshevik-Leninists. The left course of Stalin, springing from an attempt to undermine the roots of the Left Opposition, ran into the absurdity of the theory and practice of the 'third period.' The abandonment of this attack of fever, which led to the downright catastrophe of the Comintern, was once more the consequence of the criticism of the Opposition. The power of this criticism, despite the numerical weakness of the left wing, lies in general where the power of Marxism lies: in the ability to analyse, to foresee, and to point out correct roads. The faction of the Bolshevik-Leninists is consequently even now one of the most important factors in the development of the theory and practice of socialist construction in the USSR and of the international proletarian revolution.

The proletariat is not only the fundamental productive force, but also the class upon which the Soviet system and socialist construction rest. The dictatorship can have no powers of resistance if its distorted regime leads to the political indifference of the proletariat. The high rate of industrialization cannot last long if it depends on excessive strain which leads to the physical exhaustion of the workers. A constant shortage of the most necessary means of existence and a permanent state of alarm under the knout of the administration endanger the whole socialist construction. 'The dying away of inner-party democracy', says the platform of the Opposition of the USSR, 'leads to a dying away of workers' democracy in general — in the trade unions and in all the other nonparty mass organizations.' Since the publication of the platform, this process has made more ravaging advances. The trade unions have finally been degraded to auxiliary organs of the ruling bureaucracy. A system of administrative pressure has been built up, under the name of shock troops, as if it were a question of a short mountain pass and not of a great historical epoch. In spite of this, the termination of the five-year plan will find the Soviet economy before a new, still steeper ascent. With the aid of the formula 'overtaking and outstripping', the bureaucracy partly misleads itself but mainly misleads the workers in regard to the stage attained, and prepares a sharp crisis of disappointment.

The economic plan must be checked on from the point of view of the actual systematic improvement of the material and cultural conditions of the working class in town and country. The trade unions must be brought back to their basic task: the collective educator, not the knout. The proletariat in the USSR and in the rest of the world must stop being lulled by exaggerations of what has been attained and the minimizing of the tasks and the difficulties. The problem of raising the political independence of the proletariat and its initiative in all fields must be put in the foreground of the whole policy. The genuine attainment of this aim is inconceivable without a struggle against the excessive privileges of individual groups and strata, against the extreme inequality of living conditions, and, above all, against the enormous prerogatives and favoured position of the uncontrolled bureaucracy.

5. Conclusions

1. The economic successes of the USSR, which have made a way for themselves in spite of the long-lasting alliance between centrists, right-wingers, Mensheviks, and saboteurs in the field of planning, represent the greatest triumph of the socialist methods of economy and a powerful factor of the world revolution.

2. To defend the USSR, as the main fortress of the world proletariat, against all the assaults of world imperialism and of internal

counter-revolution is the most important duty of every class-conscious worker.

3. The crisis of the economic development of the USSR spring from the capitalist and precapitalist contradictions inherited from the past, as well as from the contradiction between the international character of modern productive forces and the national character of socialist construction in the USSR.

4. Built upon the lack of understanding of the latter contradiction, the theory of socialism in one country in turn appears as the source of practical mistakes, which provoke crises or deepen them.

5. The strength of the Soviet bureaucracy has unfolded on the basis of the abrupt decline in the political activity of the Soviet proletariat after a number of years of the highest exertion of forces, a series of defeats of the international revolution, the stabilization of capitalism, and the strengthening of the international social democracy.

6. Socialist construction, under the conditions of class contradictions at home and of capitalist encirclement abroad, demands a strong, farsighted, active party as the fundamental political precondition for planned economy and class manoeuvring.

7. Having reached power with the direct support of social forces hostile to the October Revolution and after the crushing of the revolutionary internationalist wing of the party, the centrist bureaucracy could nevertheless only maintains its domination by measures of suppression of party control, election, and the public opinion of the working class.

8. Now that the centrist bureaucracy has strangled the party, that is, has lost its eyes and ears, it moves along gropingly and determines its path under the direct impact of the classes, oscillating between opportunism and adventurism.

9. The course of development has completely confirmed all the essential principles of the platform of the Russian Opposition, in their critical parts as well as in their positive demands.

10. In the last period, the features of the three fundamental currents in the Communist Party of the Soviet Union and in the Communist International have emerged with particular lucidity: the Marxist-Leninist, the centrist, and the right. The tendency of ultra-leftism makes its appearance either as the crowning of one of the zigzags of centrism or at the periphery of the Left Opposition.

11. The policy and the regime of the centrist bureaucracy became the source of the most acute and direct dangers for the dictatorship of

the proletariat. The systematic struggle against ruling centrism is the most essential part of the struggle for the rehabilitation, the strengthening and the development of the first workers' state.

12. The ignoring of the material state and the political mood of the working class constitutes the most essential feature of the bureaucratic regime which, with the aid of the methods of naked command and administrative pressure, hopes to construct the realm of national socialism.

13. The bureaucratic forcing of the tempos of industrialization and collectivization, based upon a false theoretical position and not verified by the collective thought of the party, means a relentless accumulation of disproportions and contradictions, especially along the lines of the mutual relations with the world economy.

14. The property relations in the USSR, in spite of the distortions of the Soviet regime and in spite of the disastrous policy of the centrist bureaucracy, remains a workers' state.

15. The bourgeoisie could come to power in the USSR in no other way than with the aid of a counter-revolutionary upheaval. The proletarian vanguard still has the possibility of putting the bureaucracy in its place, subordinating it to its control, insuring the correct policy, and, by means of decisive and bold reforms, regenerating the party, the trade unions, and the soviets.

16. Yet, with the maintenance of the Stalinist regime, the contradictions accumulating within the framework of the official party, especially at the moment of the sharpening of the economic difficulties, must lead inevitably to a political crisis, which may raise the question of power anew in all its scope.

17. For the fate of the Soviet regime, it will be of decisive significance whether the proletarian vanguard will be in a position to stand up in time, to close its ranks, and to offer resistance to the bloc of the Thermidorean-Bonapartist forces backed by world imperialism.

18. The Left Opposition can fulfil its duty towards the proletarian vanguard only by uninterrupted critical work, by Marxist analysis of the situation, by the determination of the correct path for the economic development of the USSR and for the struggle of the world proletariat, by the timely raising of living slogans, and by intransigent struggle against the plebiscitary regime which fetters the forces of the working class.

19. The solution of these theoretical and political tasks is conceivable only under the condition that the Russian faction of the

Bolshevik-Leninists strengthens its organizations, penetrates into all the important units of the official party and other organizations of the working class, and at the same time remains an inseparable part of the International Left Opposition.

20. One of the most urgent tasks consists in making the experience of the economic construction in the USSR the object of an all-sided free study and discussion within the Commmunist Party of the Soviet Union and the Communist International.

21. The criteria for the discussion, elaboration and verification of the economic programmes, are: (a) systematic raising of the real wages of the workers; (b) closing of the scissors of industrial and agricultural prices, that is, assuring the alliance with the peasantry; (c) closing of the scissors of domestic and world prices, that is, protection of the monopoly of foreign trade against the onslaught of cheap prices; (d) raising of the quality of production, to which the same significance should be attached as to its quantity; (e) stabilization of the domestic purchasing power of the chervonets, which together with the principle of planning will for a long time to come remain a necessary element of economic regulation.

22. The administrative chase after 'maximum' tempos must give way to the elaboration of optimum (the most advantageous) tempos which do not guarantee the fulfilment of the command of the day for display purposes, but the constant growth of the economy on the basis of its dynamic equilibrium, with a correct distribution of domestic resources and a broad, planned utilization of the world market.

23. For this it is necessary above all to abandon the false perspective of a complete, self-sufficient national economic development which flows from the theory of socialism in one country.

24. The problem of the foreign trade of the USSR must be put as a key problem in the perspective of a growing connection with the world economy.

25. In harmony with this, the question of the economic collaboration of the capitalist countries with the USSR should be made one of the current slogans of all the sections of the Comintern, especially in the period of the world crisis and unemployment.

26. The collectivization of peasant farms should be adjusted in accordance with the actual initiative of the agricultural proletariat and the village poor, and their alliance with the middle peasants. A serious and all-sided re-examination of the experiences of the collective farms must be made the task of the workers and the advanced peasants. The

state programme of building collective farms must be brought into harmony with the actual results of experience and with the given technical and total economic resources.

27. The bureaucratic utopia of the 'liquidation of the kulaks as a class' in two to three years on the basis of the peasants' stocks should be rejected. A firm policy of the systematic restriction of the exploitive tendencies of the kulaks must be conducted. Toward this end, the inevitable process of differentiation within the collective farms, as well as between them, must be followed attentively, and the collective farms in no case identified with socialist enterprises.

28. Stop being guided in the economy by considerations of bureaucratic prestige: no embellishment, no concealment, no deception. Don't pass off as socialism the present transitional economy of the Soviet Union, which remains very low in the level of its productive forces and very contradictory in its structure.

29. There must be an end once and for all to the ruinous practice, unworthy of a revolutionary party, of the Roman Catholic dogma of the infallibility of the leadership.

30. The theory and practice of Stalinism must be condemned. Return to the theory of Marx and to the revolutionary methodology of Lenin.

31. The party must be re-established as the organization of the proletarian vanguard.

Regardless of the greatest economic successes on the one hand and the extreme weakening of the Comintern on the other, the revolutionary specific weight of Bolshevism on the world political map is infinitely more significant than the specific weight of the Soviet economy on the world market. While the nationalized and collectivized economy of the USSR is expanded and developed by all means possible, the correct perspective must be retained. It must not be forgotten for a minute that the overthrow of the world bourgeoisie in the revolutionary struggle is a far more real and immediate task than 'overtaking and outstripping' the world economy, without overstepping the boundaries of the USSR in doing it.

The present profound crisis of capitalist economy opens up revolutionary possibilities to the proletariat of the advanced capitalist countries. The inevitable rise in the militant activity of the working masses will sharply delineate all the problems of the revolution again, and will tear the ground from under the autocracy of the centrist bureaucracy. The Left Opposition will enter into the revolutionary period armed with a clear understanding of the road already traversed, of the mistakes already committed, of the new tasks and perspectives.

The complete and final way out of the internal and external contradictions will be found by the USSR on the arena of the victorious revolution of the world proletariat, and only there.

The Soviet Economy
in Danger

1932

Preface

The successes of the first two years of the Five Year Plan demonstrated to the bourgeoisie of the entire world that the proletarian revolution was a much more serious business than was apparent in the beginning. The interest in the Soviet 'experiment' grew apace. Conspicuous groups of eminent bourgeois publications in diverse countries began printing comparatively objective economic information.

At the same time the international Communist press played up the most optimistic estimates of the Soviet press, exaggerating them crudely, presumably in the interests of propaganda, and transforming them into an economic legend.

Petty-bourgeois democrats, who were not at all in a hurry to form an opinion about so complex a fact as the October Revolution, welcomed with glee the possibility of discovering support for their belated sympathies in the statistics of the Five Year Plan. Magnanimously, at last, they 'recognized' the Soviet Republic in reward for its economic and cultural attainments. This act of moral heroism provided many of them with an opportunity to take an interesting trip at reduced rates.

It is infinitely more deserving, forsooth, to defend the socialist construction of the first workers' state than to sustain the pretensions of Wall Street or of the City. But one can take as little stock in the lukewarm sympathies of this gentry toward the Soviet government as in the antipathies of the Amsterdam Congress toward militarism.

People after the type of the Webbs (and they are not the worst of this lot) are, naturally, not at all inclined to break their heads over the contradictions of Soviet economy. Without in any manner committing themselves, they strive chiefly to utilize the conquests of the

Soviets in order thus to shame or urge ahead the ruling circles of their land. A foreign revolution serves them as a subordinate weapon for their reformism. For this purpose, as well as for their personal peace of mind, 'the Friends of the USSR', together with the international Communist bureaucracy, require a picture of the successes in the USSR, as plain and homogeneous and as comforting as possible. Whoever disturbs this picture is none other than an enemy and a counter-revolutionist.

A crude and detrimental idealization of the transitional regime in particular has entrenched itself in the international Communist press during the last two years, that is, during that period in which the contradictions and disproportions of Soviet economy have already found their way into the pages of the official Soviet press.

There is nothing so precarious as sympathies that are based on legends and fiction. There is no depending on people who require fabrications for their sympathies. The impending crisis of Soviet economy will inevitably, and within the rather near future, crumple the sugary legend, and, we have no reason to doubt, will scatter many, and beat friends into the byways of indifference, if not of enmity.

What is much worse and much more serious is that the Soviet crisis will catch the European workers, and chiefly the Communists, utterly unprepared, and render them receptive to social-democratic criticism, which is absolutely inimical to the Soviets and to socialism.

In this question, as in all others, the proletarian revolution requires the truth, and only the truth. Within the scope of this brief pamphlet, I have deemed it necessary to present in all their acuteness the contradictions of Soviet economy, the incompleteness and the precariousness of many of its conquests, the coarse errors of the leadership and the dangers that stand in the path of socialism. Let our petty-bourgeois friends lavishly apply their pink and baby-blue colourations. We deem it more correct to mark with a heavy black line the weak and indefensible points where the enemy threatens to break through. The clamour about our enmity to the Soviet Union is so absurd as to bear within itself its own antidote. The nearest future will bring with it a new confirmation of our correctness. The Left Opposition teaches the workers to foresee dangers and not to be at a loss when they are upon us.

He who accepts the proletarian revolution only with the right conditions and lifelong guarantees, cannot continue on the road with us. We accept the workers' state as it is and we assert, 'This is our state'. Despite its heritage of backwardness, despite starvation and sluggishness, despite the bureaucratic mistakes and even abominations, the workers of the entire world must defend tooth and nail their future socialist fatherland, which is within this state.

First and foremost we serve the Soviet republic in that we tell the workers the truth about it and thereby teach them to lay the road for a better future.

Prinkipo, October 22, 1932.

Soviet Economy in Danger

The art of planning

The prerequisites for socialist planning were first laid by the October overturn and by the fundamental laws of the Soviet state. In the course of a number of years state organs of centralized management of economy were created and put in operation. Great creative work was performed. What was destroyed by the imperialist war and the civil war has been re-established. New grandiose enterprises were created, new industries, entire branches of industry. The capacity of the proletariat, organized into a state, to direct the economy by new methods and to create material values at a hitherto unheard-of pace, has been demonstrated in actuality. All this was achieved against the background of decaying world capitalism. Socialism, as a system, for the first time demonstrated its title to historic victory not on the pages of *Das Kapital* but by the praxis of hydro-electric plants and blast-furnaces. Marx, it goes without saying, would have preferred this method of demonstration.

However, light-minded assertions to the effect that the USSR has already entered into socialism are criminal. The achievements are great. But there still remains a very long and arduous road to the actual victory over economic anarchy, to the surmounting of dispro-portions, to the guarantee of the harmonious character of economic life.

Even though the first Five Year Plan took into consideration all possible angles, by the very nature of things it could not be anything but a first and a rough hypothesis, which was bound to undergo fundamental reconstruction in the process of the work. It is impossi-ble to create *a priori* a complete system of economic harmony. The

99

planning hypothesis could not but include old disproportions and the inevitability of the development of new ones. Centralized management implies not only great disadvantages but also the danger of centralizing the mistakes, that is, of elevating them to an excessively high degree. Only continuous regulation of the plan in the process of its fulfilment, its reconstruction in part and as a whole, can guarantee its economic effectiveness.

The art of socialist planning does not drop from heaven nor is it presented full-blown into one's hands with the conquest of power. This art may be attained only by struggle, step by step, not by units but by millions as an integral part of the new economy and culture. There is nothing either astonishing or disheartening in the fact that at the 15th anniversary of the October revolution the art of economic management still remains on a very low plane. The newspaper, *For Industrialization* deems it possible to announce: 'Our operative planning has neither hands nor feet' (September 12, 1932). And in the meantime, the crux of the matter is precisely in operative planning.

We have stressed more than once that, 'under incorrect planning or, what is more important, under incorrect regulation of the plan in the process of its fulfilment, a crisis may develop toward the very end of the Five Year Plan and may create insurmountable difficulties for the utilization and development of its indubitable successes' (*Bulletin of the Opposition*, No. 23, July 15, 1931). It is precisely for this reason that we considered that the hastily and purely fortuitous 'translation of the Five Year Plan into four years was an act of light-minded adventurism' (*idem*). Both our fears and our warnings have been unfortunately fully confirmed.

At the present moment there cannot even be a discussion about the actual completion of the Five Year Plan in four years (or more exactly, four years and three months). The most frantic lashing and spurring ahead in the course of the final two months will have no effect any longer on the general totals. It is as yet impossible to determine the actual percentage, that is, measured in terms of economy — of the fulfilment of the preliminary programme. The data published in the press take on more a formally statistical than an exact economic character. Should the construction of a new plant be accomplished up to 90 per cent of its completion and then the work be stopped because of the obvious lack of raw material, then from a formally statistical viewpoint one may enter the plan as fulfilled 90 per cent. But from the point of view of economy the expenses accrued must simply be entered under the column of losses. The balance sheet of the actual effectiveness (the useful functioning) of plants constructed or in the process of construction, from the viewpoint of the national economic balance, still belongs entirely to the future.

The situation on the eve of the second Five Year Plan

But the results obtained, no matter how imposing if taken by themselves — even if considered from the bald quantitative viewpoint — are far short of those sketched in the plan.

The output of coal is maintained at present on the level of last year, therefore it has far from reached the plan figures set for the *third* year of the Five Year Plan. 'The Donbas lags behind at the tail-end of the most backward branches of Soviet industry', complains *Pravda*. 'The tension in the fuel balance is on the increase', echoes *For Industrialization* (October 8, 1932).

In 1931 4.9 million tons of cast iron were produced instead of 7.9 million set by the plan; 5.3 million tons of steel instead of 8.8 million; and finally 4 million tons of rolled steel instead of 6.7 million. In comparison with 1930 this signifies a falling off in cast iron of 2 per cent, in steel of 6 per cent, in rolled steel of 10 per cent.

For nine months of 1932 there were 4.5 million tons of cast iron produced, 4.1 million tons of steel, 3.5 million tons of rolled stock. Alongside of the considerable rise in the output of iron (new blastfurnaces!) the production of steel and rolled steel in the current year remains approximately on the level of last year. From the viewpoint of the general tasks of the industrialization what decides, of course, is not the raw iron but the rolled stock and steel.

Side by side with these quantitive results, which *Economic Life* characterizes as 'shocking lapses' there are to be placed extremely unfavourable and because of their consequences, much more dangerous lapses in quality. Following the specialized economic press, *Pravda* openly confesses that in heavy metallurgy 'the situation as regards the indices of quality is impermissible'. 'The defective products eat up steel that is up to quality.' 'The cost of production of commodities is rising sharply.' Two figures will suffice: in 1931 a ton of iron cost 35 roubles; in the first half of the current year the cost came to 60 roubles.

In 1929-1930, 47 thousand tons of copper were smelted; in 1931,

48 thousand tons, one-third of the amount set by the plan. For the current year the plan has been lowered to 90 thousand tons but for the first 8 months less than 30 thousand tons have been smelted. What this means in the manufacture of machines in general and of electro-technical equipment in particular, requires no comment.

In the sphere of electrification, with all its successes, there is considerable lagging behind; the power plants in August delivered 71 per cent of the energy they were supposed to develop. *For Industriali-zation* writes about 'the inept, illiterate and the uncultured exploita-tion of the erected power stations'. Great difficulties are being threatened in the winter in the sphere of power production. They have already begun in the Moscow and Leningrad regions.

Light industry which lagged excessively behind the plan last year, showed a rise in the first half of the current year of 16 per cent but in the third quarter it fell below the figures of last year. The food industry occupies the last place. Supplementary production by heavy industrial plant over the eight months accounted for only 35 per cent of the yearly stipulation. It is not possible at present to estimate what part of this mass of commodities that are improvized in a hurry, really meets the requirements of the market.

The factories are supplied with coal and raw material at lightning speed. Industry, as *Economic Life* puts it, 'works on lightning'. But even bolts of lightning cannot deliver what does not exist.

Coal, hastily mined and poorly sorted, hampers the operation of coke-producing enterprises. Excessively high content of moisture and cinders in the coke not only reduces the quantity of produced metal by millions of tons but also lowers its quality. Machines of poor metal produce inferior products, result in break-downs, force inactivity upon the working hands, and deteriorate rapidly.

In the Urals, the paper informs us, 'the blastfurnaces are at fever-pitch'; because of inadequate supply of fuel they are allowed to cool down from 3 days to 20 days. Here is a circumstance illuminating to the highest degree: the metallurgical plants in the Urals had their own horse convoys for the transportation of fuel; in February of this year the horses numbered 27,000, the number fell in July to 14,000; and in September to 4,000. The reason for it is lack of fodder.

Pravda characterizes in the following manner the condition of the Stalingrad tractor factory in which the quantity of annual castings fell from 250,000 tons to 140,000 . 'The equipment, due to the absence of rudimentary and constant technical supervision . . . has excessively deteriorated.' 'Defective products have become as high as 35 per cent.' 'The entire mechanism of the corporation is wallowing in dirt.' 'In the foundries there is never a thought of the next day.' 'Methods of handicraft are swamping conveyor belt production.'

Why is production lowered in light metallurgy in the face of colossal investments? Because, replies *Pravda*, 'the separate branches of a single combine are not co-ordinated with one another in their capacity.' And in the meantime the task of co-ordinating branches has been solved by capitalist technology. And how much more complex and difficult is the question of interco-ordination of independent enterprises and entire branches of industry.

'The cement factory in Podolsk is in dangerous straits', writes *For Industrialization*: 'In the first half year the production programme was fulfilled approximately 60 per cent, in the last months the fulfilment dropped to 40 per cent . . . The basic costs are twice as high as those set by the plan.' The characteristics cited above apply in various degrees to the entire present industry.

The administrative hue and cry after quantity leads to a frightful lowering of quality; low quality undermines on the next stage the struggle for quantity; the ultimate cost of economically irrational 'successes' surpasses as a rule many times the value of these same successes. Every advanced worker is acquainted with this dialectic not through the books of the Communist academy (alas! more inferior goods) but in practice, through experience in their own mines, factories, railroads, fuel stations etc.

The consequences of the frenzied chase have permeated in all their entirety the sphere of education. *Pravda* is compelled to admit that, 'by lowering the quality of preparation, by skipping scientific subjects, or by passing over them at 'cavalry trot', the VTUZI (Highest Technological Educational Institutions) that took this path, instead of aiding industry, injured it.' But, indeed, who is responsible for the 'cavalry trot' in the highest educational institutions?

If we were to introduce a corrective coefficient for quality into the official data, then the indices of the fulfilment of the plan would immediately suffer substantial drops. Even Kuybishev was forced to admit this more than a year ago. 'The figures relating to the tremendous growth of industry become relative', he announced cautiously at the session of the Supreme Soviet Economic Council, 'if one takes into account the variations in quality'. Rakovsky expressed himself much more lucidly: 'If one does not take into account the quality of production then the quantitative indices are nothing but statistics.'

Capital reconstruction

More than two years ago, Rakovsky warned that the scope of the plan was beyond the available resources. 'Neither the scale of the growth of production specified by the plan', he wrote, 'nor the specified plan of capital construction were prepared for . . . The entire preceding policy in the sphere of industry reduced itself in reality to the forced exploitation of old fixed capital . . . without the slightest concern for the future.' The attempt to compensate for lapses by a single leap ahead is least realistic in the sphere of capital construction. The resources necessary for the fulfilment of the plan 'do not obtain in the country and will not obtain in the near future'. Hence the warning: 'the plan of capital construction will break down in a considerable measure'.

And this prediction also has been completely substantiated. In the sphere of construction the lag was extremely great as early as 1931. It has grown still more in the current year. The transport construction programme for 9 months was fulfilled 38 per cent according to the estimates of the department itself. In other branches the matters relating to construction are as a general rule even less favourable; and worst of all is the sphere of housing construction. The material and monetary resources are divided between altogether too many constructions, which leads to low effectiveness of the investment.

Sixty five million roubles were expended on the Balashaisky copper factory, the expenses continue to grow from day to day — actually all for nothing; in order to continue work it was necessary to transport in the course of a year 300 thousand tons of freight, whereas the ready transport provides all told only 20 thousand tons. Examples of a similar kind, though not of such clarity, are all too many.

The poor quality of materials and of equipment reacts most cruelly on capital construction. 'Iron for roofing is of such rotten quality,' writes *Pravda*, 'that it cracks when once handled.'

The shocking lagging behind in the sphere of capital undertakings automatically undermines the foundations of the second five year plan.

The problem of the proportionality of the elements of production and the branches of economy constitutes the very heart of socialist economy. The tortuous roads that lead to the solution of this problem are not charted on any map. To discover them — or more correctly to lay them — is the work of a lengthy and arduous future.

The whole of industry groans from the lack of spare parts. Weavers' looms remain inactive because a bolt is not to be had. 'The assortment of articles produced', writes EJ, 'in the line of commodities of wide-spread consumption is haphazard and does not correspond to . . . the demand.'

'One billion roubles has been immobilized, "frozen" by (heavy) industry, in the course of only the first half of 1932, in the form of stocks of materials, unfinished products and even finished goods in factory warehouses.' (*For Industrialization*, September 12, 1932). Such are the expressions in terms of money of certain disproportions and discordances according to the official estimate.

Major and minor disproportions call forth the need of turning to the international market. Imported goods to the value of one *chervonetz* can bring out of its moribund state home production to the value of hundreds and thousands of *chervontzi*. The general growth of economy, on the one hand, and the sprouting up of new demands and new disproportions, on the other, invariably increase the need for linking up with the world economy. The programme of 'independence' that is, of the self-sufficient character of Soviet economy, discloses more and more its reactionary and utopian character. Autarchy is the ideal of Hitler, and not of Marx and Lenin.

Thus the import of ore from the inception of the Five Year Plan multiplied five times in volume and four times in value. If within the current year this article of import fell off, it was exclusively on account of the foreign exchange. But on this account the import of factory machinery grew excessively.

Kaganovich in a speech on October 8, asserted that the Opposition, Left as well as Right, 'proposes to us that we strengthen our dependence upon the capitalist world'. As if the matter concerned some artificial and arbitrary step, and not the automatic logic of economic growth!

At the same time the Soviet press cites with praise the interview given by Sokolnikov on the eve of his departure from London. 'In England there is increasingly widespread recognition of the fact that the *advanced* position of the Soviet state in industry and technology will present in itself a *much wider* market for the products of British industry.' As a sign of the economic progress of the Soviet Union, Sokolnikov considers not the weakening but the strengthening of the ties with the foreign market, and consequently the strengthening of the dependence upon world economy. Is it possible that the former Oppositionist Sokolnikov is trading in 'Trotskyist contraband'? But if so, why is he being screened by the official press?

The position of the workers

Stalin's speech (in July 1931) with its salutary 'six conditions' was directed against the low quality of production, the high basic cost, the migration of labouring forces, the high percentage of waste, etc. From that time on there has not appeared an article without reference to 'the historic speech'. And in the meantime all these ailments which were to be cured by the six conditions have become aggravated and have assumed a more malignant character.

From day to day the official press bears witness to the failure of Stalin's prescription. In explanation of the falling off in production *Pravda* points out 'the decrease in labour power in factories, the growing migration, the weakening of labour discipline' (September 23). In the category of reasons for the extremely low productivity of the Red Ural combine, *For Industrialization*, alongside of 'the shocking disproportions between the different parts of the combine' lists the following (1) 'the enormous migration of labour forces'; (2) 'the dunder-headed policy of the working wage' (3) 'failure to provide (the millworkers) with some manner of liveable quarters'; (4) 'the indescribable food for the millworkers'; (5) 'the catastrophic falling off of labour discipline'. We have quoted word for word. As regards the migration, which 'has grown beyond all bounds', this same paper writes, 'the living conditions (of the workers) are ghastly in all the enterprises of non-ferrous metallurgy without exception.'

In the locomotive factories which failed to provide the country with about 250 locomotives for the first three-quarters of the year, 'there is to be observed an acute insufficiency of skilled workers. More than 2,000 workers in the course of the summer left from the Kolomensk factory alone'. The reasons? 'Bad living conditions'. In the Sormovsk factory — 'the factory kitchen is a dive of the worst sort.' (*For Industrialization*, September 28). In the privileged tractor factory in Stalingrad, 'the factory kitchen has fallen sharply in its work'

(*Pravda*, September 21). To what a pitch the dissatisfaction of the workers must have risen in order to force these facts into the columns of the Stalinist press!

In the textile industry, naturally, conditions are not better. 'In the Ivanovsk district alone', EL informs us, 'about 35,000 qualified weavers left the enterprises.' According to the words of this same paper, there are enterprises to be found in the country in which more than 60 per cent of the total work force changes every month. 'The factory is turning into a thoroughfare'.

In explanation of the cruel flop of 'the six conditions' there was for a long time a tendency to confine the observations to bald accusations against the management and the workers themselves, 'incapacity', 'lack of willingness', 'resting on their laurels', etc. However, for the last few months the papers more and more often point out, mostly on the sly, the actual core of the evil, the unbearable living conditions of the workers.

Rakovsky pointed out this reason of reasons more than two years ago . . . 'The reason for the increase in breakdowns, the reason for the falling in labour discipline, the reason for the need to increase the number of workers', he wrote, 'lies in the fact that the worker is physically incapable of bearing up under a load that overtaxes his strength.'

But why are the living conditions bad? The papers refer in explanation to 'the contemptuous (!) attitude to the questions relating to the living conditions of the workers and to providing them with the necessities of life.' (*For Industrialization*, September 24). With this single expression the Stalinist press has said more than it had intended. 'A contemptuous attitude' to the needs of the workers in the workers' state is possible only on the part of *an arrogant and uncontrolled bureaucracy*.

This risky explanation was made necessary, no doubt, in order to hide the basic fact: the direct lack of material goods to supply the workers. The national income is incorrectly distributed. Economic tasks are being set without any account being taken of the actual means. An increasingly inhuman load is being dumped on the shoulders of the workers.

References to 'breaks' in the supply of foodstuffs are now to be met with in every number of the Soviet press. Malnutrition plus forced exertions. The combination of these two conditions is enough to do away with the equipment and to exhaust the producers themselves. In consolation, *Pravda* prints a photograph of a working woman in the act of feeding 'her own private' pig. That is precisely the way out. 'Private domestic economy', lectures the paper (October 3), 'hitherto tied the worker to capitalism but now it attaches him to the Soviet system.' One cannot believe one's eyes! Once upon a time we learned that private domestic economy depends upon the enslavement of the woman, the most abominable element of social slavery in general. But now it appears that 'its own private' pig attaches the proletariat to socialism. Thus the hypocritical functionaries turn cruel necessity into virtue.

Poor nourishment and nervous fatigue engender an apathy to the surrounding environment. As a result, not only the old factories but also the new ones that have been built according to the last word in technology, fall quickly into a moribund state. *Pravda* itself issues the following challenge, 'Try and find at least one blast furnace that is not wallowing in rubbish!'

As regards conditions of morale, they are no better than the physical conditions. 'The management of the factory has become cut off from the masses' (*Pravda*). Instead of a sensitive approach to the workers, there obtain 'bare-faced commanding and domineering.' In every individual instance the matter touches isolated factories. *Pravda* cannot guess that the sum of the individual cases constitutes the Stalinist regime.

In the entire non-ferrous metal industry, 'there is not a single factory committee that functions more or less satisfactorily' (*For Industrialization*, September 13). However, how and why is it that in a workers' state the factory committees — of the entire industry and not only in the branch of non-ferrous metals — function unsatisfactorily? Is it not, perhaps, because they are strangled by the party bureaucracy?

At the Dzerzhinsky locomotive plant, during a single session of the nucleus bureau of the blacksmiths, there were taken up simultaneously 18 cases of expulsions from the party; in the wheelwrights — 9 cases; in the boilermakers — 12 cases. The matter is not restricted to an isolated factory. Commandeering reigns everywhere. And the sole answer of the bureaucracy to the initiative and criticism from below is — repression.

The draft of the Platform of the International Left Opposition proclaims, 'The living standards of the workers and their role in the state are the highest criterions of socialist successes.' 'If the Stalinist bureaucracy had approached the tasks of planning and of the living regulation of economy from this viewpoint', we wrote more than a year ago, 'it would not have missed fire frightfully each time, it would not have been compelled to put through the policies of wasteful zig-zags, and it would not have been placed face to face with political dangers.' (*Bulletin* 23, page 5.)

Rural economy

'The rural economy of the Soviet Union', wrote *Pravda* on September 28, 'has become absolutely intrenched on the road to Socialism.' Such phrases, bolstered up as a rule by bare citations of the number of collectivized homesteads and hectares, represent in themselves a hollow mockery of the actual condition of the rural economy and of the inter-relations between the city and the village.

The headlong chase after breaking records in collectivization, without taking any account of the economic and cultural potentialities of the rural economy, has led in actuality to ruinous consequences. It has destroyed the stimuli of the small commodity producer long before it was able to supplant them by other and much higher economic stimuli. Administrative pressure, which exhausts itself quickly in industry, turns out to be absolutely powerless in the sphere of rural economy.

'The village of Caucasus', we are informed by this same *Pravda*, 'was awarded the prize for its spring sowing campaign. Concurrently, the tillage turned out to be so poor that the fields were entirely overgrown by weeds.' The village of Caucasus is a symbol of the administrative hue and cry after quantity in the domain of rural economy. 100 per cent collectivization has resulted in 100 per cent overgrowth of weeds on the fields.

The kolkhozes were allotted more than 100,000 tractors. A gigantic victory! But as the innumerable local newspaper reports show, the effectiveness of the tractors far from corresponds to their number. At the Poltava machine-building station, one of the newest, 'out of 27 tractors recently delivered, 19 are already seriously damaged'. These figures do not hold only for exceptional cases. The station on the Volga Ukraine has 52 tractors; of these, two have been out of operation since spring, 14 were being completely overhauled, and of the remaining 36, less than half are being utilized in sowing, 'and even

these remain alternately idle.' The coefficient of the useful functioning of the 100,000 tractors has not been determined as yet!

During the dizziest moment of 100 per cent collectivization,
Rakovsky made a stern diagnosis, 'In the sum total of the results
which have been prepared for by the entire preceding policies and
which have been aggravated by the period of ultra-Left adventurism,
the chief result will be the lowering of the productive forces of the
rural economy, indubitably evident in the sphere of stock-raising and
partly so in the cultivation of raw materials for industry, and becoming increasingly evident in the sphere of the cultivation of grain.'

Was Rakovsky mistaken? Unfortunately, no. Nothing can produce
so shocking an impression as the small, quite imperceptible, decree
issued by the CEC on September 11, 1932, which met with no
comments in the Soviet press. Under the signature of Kalinin and
Molotov, the individual peasant proprietors are *duty-bound* to relin-
quish, for the needs of the kolkhozes and at their request, all horses
for a stipulated price. The kolkhozes are in turn obliged to return the
horses to their owners in 'good condition'.

Such is the inter-relation between the socialist and petty-bourgeois
sections of rural economy! The kolkhozes which cultivate 80-90 per
cent of the arable lands and which should, in theory, attract the
individualists by their achievements, are compelled in actuality to
resort to the legal aid of the state in order to obtain through compulsion horses from individual proprietors for their own needs. Everything here is topsy-turvy. This single decree of September 11 represents a death sentence on the policies of Stalin-Molotov.

Could the inter-relations between the city and the village become
improved on the basis of material production?

Let us recall once again: the economic foundation of the dictatorship of the proletariat can be considered fully assured only from that
moment when the State is not forced to resort to administrative
measures of compulsion as touches the majority of the peasantry in
order to obtain the products of rural economy; that is, when in return
for machines, tools and objects for personal use, the peasants volun-
tarily supply the state with the necessary quantity of food-stuffs and
raw material. Only on this basis — along with other necessary conditions, internally as well as internationally — can collectivization
obtain a true socialist character.

The correlation between the prices for the products of industry and
the products of rural economy has changed indubitably in favour of

the peasant. In truth, it is an unfeasible task, to perform an accounting in this sphere that corresponds in some manner to reality. For instance *Pravda* writes that 'the cost of a quintal of milk ranges in the kolkhozes from 43 to 206 roubles.' The variation is even greater between the State prices and the price on the legalized markets. No less heterogeneous are the prices for the industrial products, all depending upon the channel through which they reach the peasant. But, without in any way claiming to be exact, it is possible to assert that the price-scissors, in the narrow meaning of the term, have been closed by the peasants. For its own products, the village has begun to obtain such a quantity of monetary equivalents, as would assure it industrial goods, at fixed state prices . . . if such goods were to be obtained.

But one of the most important disproportions consists in the fact that the availability of commodities does not correspond to the availability of money. In the language of monetary circulation, that is what is called inflation. In the language of planned economy this signifies exaggerated plans, incorrect division of forces and means, in particular, between the production of objects for consumption and the production of means of production.

From that time when the correlation of prices began to turn against the city, the latter safe-guarded itself by 'freezing' the goods, that is, they were simply not put into circulation, but kept in hand to be distributed bureaucratically. This signified that only the pecuniary shadow of the scissors had closed its blades, while their material disproportion still remained. But the peasant is little interested in shadows. The absence of commodities has pushed him and continues to push him in the direction of a strike in cereals: he does not want to part with his grain for money.

Not having become a matter of simple and profitable exchange for both sides, the provision of foodstuffs and agricultural raw material has remained as hitherto 'a political campaign', 'militant drive', requiring each time the mobilization of the State and party apparatus. 'Many kolkhozes,' *Pravda* cautiously reports (September 26), 'resist the collection of grain, hiding their stocks.' We know what the word 'many' signifies in such a context. If the exchange between the village and the city were advantageous, then the peasants would have no cause whatever to 'hide their stocks'; but if the exchange is not advantageous, that is, if it takes the form of compulsory transfer, then *all* the kolkhozes, and not 'many' as well as the individual proprietors will strive to hide away their grain. The duties of the peasants in supplying meat provisions are officially invested at present with the character of a natural tax in kind, with all the ensuing repressive consequences. The economic results of the 100 per cent collectiviza-tion are designated much more correctly by these facts than by the bald statistics of collectivized hectares.

The fact that severe laws were passed against spoliation of socialist property sufficiently characterizes the extent of the evil, the gist of which, in the village, consists in the fact that the peasant strives to direct his grain not into the socialist, but the capitalist channels. The prices on the speculative market are high enough to justify the rise of capital punishment. What part of the foodstuffs is diverted into the channels of speculation?

In the Volga-Caspian fish trust, it is reckoned that 20 per cent of the catch goes to the private market. 'And how much really does go?' asks *Pravda* sceptically. In the rural economy the percentage of the drain should be considerably higher. But even 20 per cent means hundreds of millions of poods of bread. Repressions may become inevitable measures of self-preservation. But they cannot replace the establish-ment of the link, they do not create the economic foundation for the dictatorship of the proletariat, and they do not even guarantee the provision of foodstuffs.

The authorities, therefore, could not stop merely with repressions alone. In the struggle for foodstuffs and raw materials they found themselves compelled to order the city to liberate the village. While in the cities, particularly in the provinces, the State and co-operative stores have become depleted.

The balance of 'the link' with the village during this year has not as yet been taken. But the trading channels of the cities are exhausted. 'We gave more goods to the village', said Kaganovich in Moscow on October 8, 'and, if I may use the expression, we have offended the city.' The expression is absolutely permissible; the cities and indus-trial districts have been offended, that is, the workers.*

---

* In 1929, Preobrazhensky, justifying his capitulation, prophesied that with the aid of the Sovkhozes and Kolkhozes the party would force the kulak to his knees within two years. Four years have elapsed. And what have we? If not the kulak — he has been 'put out of commission' — then the strong middleman has forced Soviet trade to its knees, compelling it to offend the workers. As we see it, Preobrazhensky himself, in any event, was much too hasty in getting down on his knees before the Stalinist bureaucracy.

The conditions and methods of planned economy

What kind of institutions are there for constructing and applying the plan? What are the methods of checking and regulating it? What are the conditions for its success?

Three systems must be subjected in this connection to a brief analysis: (1) special state organs, that is, the hierarchical system of *plan commissions*, in the centre, as well as locally; (2) *trade*, as a system of market regulation; (3) *Soviet democracy*, as a system of living reaction of the masses upon the structure of the economy.

If there existed the universal mind, that projected itself into the scientific fancy of Laplace; a mind that would register simultaneously all the processes of nature and of society, that could measure the dynamics of their motion, that could forecast the results of their inter-reactions, such a mind, of course, could *a priori* draw up a faultless and an exhaustive economic plan, beginning with the number of hectares of wheat and down to the last button for a vest. In truth, the bureaucracy often conceives that just such a mind is at its disposal; that is why it so easily frees itself from the control of the market and of Soviet democracy. But, in reality, the bureaucracy errs frightfully in its appraisal of its spiritual resources. In its creativeness, it is obliged perforce, in actual performance, to depend upon the proportions (and with equal justice one may say, the disproportions) it has inherited from capitalist Russia; upon the data of the economic structure of contemporary capitalist nations; and finally, upon the experience of successes and mistakes of the Soviet economy itself. But even the most correct combination of all these elements will allow only of constructing a most imperfect wire skeleton of a plan, and not more.

The innumerable living participants in the economy, State as well as private, collective as well as individual, must give notice of their needs and of their relative strength not only through the statistical determinations of plan commissions but by the direct pressure of supply and demand. The plan is checked and, to a considerable measure, realized through the market. The regulation of the market itself must depend upon the tendencies that are brought out through its medium. The blueprints produced by the offices must demonstrate their economic expediency through commercial calculation.

The system of transitional economy is unthinkable without the control of the rouble. This presupposes, in its turn, that the rouble is at par. Without a firm monetary unit, commercial accounting can only increase the chaos.

The processes of economic construction are not as yet taking place within a classless society. The questions relating to the allotment of the national income compose the central shaft of the plan. It shifts with the direct development of the class struggle and that of social groups, and among them, the various strata of the proletariat itself. These are the most important social and economic questions: the link between the city and the village, that is, the balance between that which industry obtains from rural economy and that which it supplies to it; the interrelation between accumulation and consumption, between the fund for capital construction and the fund for labour wages; the regulation of wages for various categories of labour (skilled and unskilled workers, government employees, specialists, the managing bureaucracy); and finally the allotment of that share of national income which falls to the village, between the various strata of the peasantry — all these questions by their very nature do not allow of the *a priori* decisions of the bureaucracy, that has fenced itself off from the interference of interested millions.

The struggle between living interests, as the fundamental factor of planning, leads us into the domain of *politics*, which is concentrated economics. The instrument of the social groups of Soviet society are (should be): the Soviets, the trade unions, the co-operatives, and first of all the ruling party. Only through the inter-action of the three elements, State planning, the market, and Soviet democracy, can be realized the correct management of the economy of the transitional epoch, and only thus can be assured — not the complete surmounting of contradictions and disproportions within a few years (this is Utopia!) — but their mitigation, and, through just that, the strengthening of the material bases of the dictatorship of the proletariat until the moment when a new and victorious revolution will widen the arena of socialist planning and will reconstruct the system.

The need for introducing the NEP, the restoration of market relationships, was determined in its time first of all by the existence of 25 million independent peasant proprietors. This does not mean, however, that collectivization even in its first stage leads to the liquidation of the market. Collectivization becomes a living factor only to the extent to which it leaves in force the personal interest of the members of kolkhozes, by moulding their mutual relations, as well as the relations between the kolkhozes and the outside world, on the foundation of commercial calculation. This means that the correct, and economically sound, collectivization, at the given stage should lead not to the elimination of the NEP, but to a gradual reorganization of its methods.

The bureaucracy, however, went the whole way; at first, it might have appeared to it that it was taking the road of least resistance. The genuine and indubitable successes of the centralized efforts of the proletariat were identified by it with the successes of its *a priori* planning. Or to put it differently: it identified the socialist revolution with itself. By administrative collectivization it masked the unsolved problem of establishing the link with the village. Bucking up against disproportions through the NEP, it liquidated the NEP. In place of market methods it enlarged the methods of compulsion.

The stable currency unit, in the form of the *chervonetz*, constituted the most important weapon of the NEP. While in its state of dizziness, the bureaucracy decided that it was already standing firmly with both feet on the soil of economic harmony; and that the successes of today automatically guaranteed the progression of subsequent successes; and that the *chervonetz* was not a bridle that checked the sweep of the plan but on the contrary provided an independent source of capital funds. Instead of regulating the material elements of the economic process the bureaucracy began to patch up the holes by means of printing presses. In other words, it took to the road of 'optimistic' inflation.

After the administrative suppression of the NEP, the celebrated 'six conditions of Stalin' — economic accounting, piecework wages, etc. — became transformed into an empty collection of words. Economic accounting is unthinkable without market relations. The *chervonetz* is the yardstick of the link. Of what possible use for the workers are a few extra roubles a month, if he is compelled to purchase in the open market the necessities of life he lacks at ten times their price?

The restoration of open markets came as an admission of the inopportune liquidation of the NEP, but an admission that is empirical, partial, thoughtless and contradictory. To label the open markets as a form of 'Soviet' (socialist?) trade, in contrast to private trade and speculation is to practice self-imposture. Open market trading, even on the part of the kolkhoz, taken as a whole, turns out to be speculation on the required necessities for the nearest city and by its consequences leads to social differentiation, that is, to the enrichment of the minority of the more fortunately situated kolkhozes. But the chief place in the open market is occupied not by the kolkhozes but by individual members of the kolkhozes, along with the independent proprietors. The trading of the members of the kolkhozes, who sell their surplus at speculative prices leads to the differentiation within the kolkhozes. Thus the open market develops centrifugal forces within the 'socialist' village.

By eliminating the market and by installing instead Asiatic bazaars the bureaucracy has created, to consummate all else, the conditions for the most barbaric gyrations of prices, and consequently has placed a mine both under the plan and under commercial calculation. As a result, the economic chaos has been redoubled.

Parallel to this, there has gone on the ossification of the trade unions, the Soviets, and the party, which did not start yesterday. Bucking up against the friction between the city and the village, against the demands from the side of various sections of the peasantry and from the side of the proletariat, the bureaucracy ever more decisively forbade any demands, protest and criticism whatsoever. The sole prerogative, which it ultimately left to the workers, was the right to exceed production tasks. Every attempt to influence economic management from below, is immediately assigned to a deviation either to the Right or to the Left, that is, it is practically made a capital offence. The bureaucratic upper-crust, when all is said and done, has pronounced itself infallible in the sphere of socialist planning (disregarding the fact that its collaborators and inspirers turned out often to be inimical machinators and saboteurs). Thus was liquidated the basic mechanism of socialist construction — the pliant and elastic system of *Soviet democracy*. Face to face with economic reality and its difficulties the bureaucracy turned out to be armed only with the twisted and rumpled wire carcass of the plan and with its own administrative will, also considerably rumpled.

The crisis of Soviet economy

Had the general economic level, set by the first Five Year Plan, been realized only 50 per cent, this in itself could have given no cause as yet for alarm. The danger lies not in the slowing down of growth, but in the growing lack of conformity between the various branches of economy. Even if all the integral elements of the plan had been fully co-ordinated *a priori*, the lowering of the coefficient of growth by 50 per cent would by itself have engendered great difficulties because of the consequences; it is one thing to produce one million pairs of shoes instead of two millions; but it is quite another thing to finish building one half of a shoe factory. But reality is much more complex and conʦradictory than our hypothetical example. Disproportions are inherited from the past. Stipulations which are made by plan include in ᵗʰᵉmselves inevitable mistakes and miscalculations. The unfulfilment ᵤᵤ ᵢhe plaᵤ does not occur proportionately, due to the particular causes in each individual instance. The average growth of 50 per cent in the economy may mean that in sphere A the plan is fulfilled 90 per cent, whereas in sphere B, only 10 per cent; if A depends on B, then in the subsequent cycle of production, the branch A may be reduced below 10 per cent.

Consequently the misfortune does not lie in the fact that the impossibility of adventuristic tempos has been revealed. The whole trouble is that the prize leaps in industrialization have brought the diverse elements of the plan into a dire contradiction with each other. The trouble is that the economy functions without material reserves and without calculation. The trouble is that the social and political instruments for the determination of the effectiveness of the plan have been broken or mangled. The trouble is that the accrued disproportions threaten ever bigger and bigger surprises. The trouble is that the uncontrolled bureaucracy has tied up its prestige with the subsequent accumulation of errors. The trouble is that a crisis is impending with a trail of consequences such as the enforced shutting down of enterprises and unemployment.

The difference between the socialist and capitalist tempos of industrial development — even if one takes for comparison, the former progressive capitalism — is of astonishing extent. But it would be a mistake to consider as final the Soviet tempos of the last few years. The average coefficient of capitalist growth results not only from periods of expansion but also from those of crisis. Matters are otherwise with Soviet economy. In the course of the last 8-9 years it has experienced the period of uninterrupted growth. It has not as yet succeeded in working out its average indices.

Of course, we shall be told in refutation that we are transferring over to the socialist economy the laws of capitalism; that a planned economy does not require regulation by means of crises, or even, by means of premeditated lowering of tempos. The arsenal of proofs at the disposal of the Stalinist bureaucracy and its theoreticians is so restricted that it is always possible to forecast beforehand what particular generalization they will resort to. In the given instance, the matter concerns pure tautology. The fact is that we have entered into socialism and therefore we must always act 'socialistically', that is, we must regulate the economy so as to obtain ever increasing planned expansion. But the gist of the matter lies in the fact that we have not entered into socialism. We have far from attained mastery of the methods of planned regulation. We are fulfilling only the first rough hypothesis, fulfilling it poorly, and with our headlights not on as yet. Crises are not only possible as far as we are concerned, but they are inevitable. And the impending crisis has already been prepared for by the bureaucracy.

The laws that govern the transitional society are quite different from those that govern capitalism. But no less do they differ from the future laws of socialism, that is, of harmonious economy, growing on the basis of tried, proven and guaranteed dynamic equilibrium. The productive advantage of socialism, centralization, concentration, the unified spirit of management — are incalculable. But under incorrect application, particularly under bureaucratic misuse, they may turn into their opposites. And in part they have already become transformed, for the crisis now impends. Any attempt to force the economy by further lashing and spurring ahead is an attempt to redouble the misfortunes ensuing.

It is impossible to foretell the limits that the crisis will attain. The superiorities of a planned economy remain during crises as well, and one may say, they evince themselves with special clarity precisely in a crisis. Capitalist governments are compelled to wait passively until the crisis spends itself on the backs of the people, or to resort to financial hocus-pocus in the manner of von Papen. The workers' state meets the crisis as well with all its resources. All the dominant levers — the budget, credit, industry, trade — are concentrated in a single hand. The crisis may be mitigated and afterwards overcome not by bellowing commands but by measures of economic regulation. After the adventuristic offensive, it is necessary to perform a planned retreat, thought out as fully as possible. This is the task of the coming year, the sixteenth year of the proletarian dictatorship. *Il faut reculer pour mieux sauter*: Let us retreat in order the better to advance.

The official press now prints from issue to issue an uninterrupted list of accusations against the workers, the directors, the technicians, managers, co-operative personnel, and the trade unionists: all guilty of not fulfilling the plans, the instructions and 'the six conditions'. But where are the causes for this? Objective causes do not obtain. To blame for it all is the ill will of those entrusted with the fulfilling. And that is just what *Pravda* writes: 'Do there obtain any objective causes whatever for this deterioration in the work? None whatever!' (October 2, 1932). People simply do not want to work as they should — and that's all there is to it. The October plenum of the CEC has ascertained that 'there is unsatisfactory management in every link down the line.' Except, of course, that link which is called the Central Executive Committee.

But are there really no objective causes for the poor quality of the workmanship? A specified amount of time is required not only for the ripening of wheat but also for familiarization with the complex technological processes. Psychological processes, it is true, are more pliable than those of vegetation, but this pliability has its limits. One cannot skip over them. And in addition — and this is no less important — one cannot demand the maximum of intensity under minimum of nourishment.

The resolution of the October plenum of the CEC accuses the workers and the administrators of their inability 'to clinch' their highest achievements, and of their continual falling below the marks they had set. In reality, the breakdowns were ingrained in the character of the achievement themselves. By virtue of an exceptional effort a man can lift a weight that is far above his 'average' strength. But he cannot long sustain such a load over his head. It is absurd to accuse him of his inability 'to clinch' his effort.

The Soviet economy is in danger! It is not difficult to determine its ailment. It springs from the nature of the successes themselves. From an excessive and poorly calculated strain *the economy has suffered a rupture*. One must proceed to cure, painstakingly and perseveringly. Rakovsky warned us as early as 1930, 'We are entering an entire epoch, which will pass under the heading of payment in full for the entire past.'

The second Five Year Plan

The second Five Year Plan was fashioned in the scales of 'gigantism'.* It is difficult, to be more correct, it is impossible to judge 'by sight' the extent to which the final indices of the second Five Year Plan are exaggerated. But the question now touches not the balance of the Second Five Year Plan, but its points of departure, the line of its juncture with the first Five Year Plan. The first year of the second Five Year Plan has received an onerous inheritance from the last year of the first Five Year Plan.

The second plan, according to the design, is the spiral continuation of the first plan. But the first plan has not been brought to completion. The second plan from the very beginning is left suspended in mid-air. If one leaves things to go on as they have been, then the second Five Year Plan will begin by patching up the holes of the first under the administrative whip. This means that the crisis will be aggravated. In this manner one brings matters to a catastrophe.

There is only one way out: *the inauguration of the Second Five Year Plan must be put off for one year*. 1933 must be made a buffer between the first Five Year Plan and the second. In the course of this period it is necessary on the one hand, to verify the inheritance left by the first Five Year Plan, to fill in the most yawning gaps, to mitigate the unbearable disproportions and to straighten out the economic front; and on the other hand, to reconstruct the Second Five Year Plan, so calculating it as to make its points of departure about equal to the actual and not imaginary results of the first Five Year Plan.

Doesn't this simply mean that the period for the completion of the first plan will be prolonged another year? No, unfortunately that is not the case. The material consequences of the four years' of hue and cry cannot be stricken out from reality by one stroke of a pen. A careful checking over is necessary, a regulation, and a determination of the coefficients of growth actually achieved. The present condition of economy excludes in general any possibility of planned work. 1933 cannot be a supplementary year of the first Five Year Plan, nor the

---

* The hostility, an outright hatred, toward 'gigantism' is rapidly growing in Soviet circles, as a natural and an inevitable reaction against the adventurism of the last period. There is no need, however, to explain to what extent this reaction, from which the petty-bourgeois skinflint spirit derives satisfaction, may in the future become dangerous to the socialist construction.

first year of the second. It must occupy an independent position between the two, in order to assure the mitigation of the consequences of adventurism and the preparation of the material and moral prerequisites for planned expansion.

The Left Opposition in its own time was the first to demand the inauguration of the Five Year Plan. Now it is duty bound to say: It is necessary to put off the second Five Year Plan. Away with shrieking enthusiasm! Away with stock jobbing! There is no reconciling them with planned activity. Then, you are for retreat? Yes, for a temporary retreat. And what about the prestige of the infallible leadership? The fate of the dictatorship of the proletariat is more important than blown-up prestige.

Having been knocked off balance, the Soviet economy is in need of serious reconstruction. Under capitalism the broken equilibrium is restored by the blind forces of the crisis. The socialist republic allows of applying conscious and rational cures.

It is impossible, of course, to halt production in the whole country as it is halted during repairs in a factory or in an enterprise. But there is also no need whatever for it. It is enough to lower the tempos. The current productive labour for 1933 cannot be carried on without a plan, but this plan must be one for a single year, worked out on the basis of moderate quality quotas.

Attainments in quality must be given first place. Inopportune constructions should be liquidated; all forces and resources must be concentrated upon constructions of the first rank; the inter-relations between the various branches of industry must be balanced on the basis of experience; factories must be put in order; equipment must be restored.

Let there be an end to driving and spurring, and establishing records, but let the productivity of each enterprise be subjected to its technological rhythm. Return to the laboratories whatever has been taken too soon from out of the laboratories. Finish building whatever still remains unfinished. Straighten out whatever has been bent. Repair that which has been damaged. Prepare the factory for a transition to the highest stage. Quality quotas must be given a character both supple and conditional in order that they may not interfere with achievements in quantity.

1933 must gain complete mastery over the labour turn-over, by bettering the conditions of the workers; that's where the beginning must be made, for here is to be found the key to everything else.

Workers and their families must be assured of food, shelter and clothing. No matter what the price!

The management and the proletarian cadres of factories should be freed of supplementary burdens, such as the planting of potatoes, breeding rabbits, etc. All questions relating to supplying factories with necessities must be regulated as independent and not supplementary tasks.

Order must be brought into the production of objects for mass consumption. Commodities must be adapted to human needs and not to the raw by-products of the heavy industry.

The process of inflation must be stopped with an iron hand and the stable monetary unit must be restored. This difficult and painful operation cannot be undertaken without boldly curtailing capital investments, without sacrificing many hundred millions that have been inexpediently or inopportunely sunk in new constructions, in order that losses amounting to billions may be forestalled in the future.

A temporary retreat is necessary both in industry and in rural economy. The furthermost line of the retreat cannot be determined beforehand. It will be revealed only in the experience of capital reconstruction.

The managing organs must control, assist, and pick out everything that is capable of living and functioning, but they should desist from driving enterprises to their doom, as is the case now. The economy and the human beings need a breathing spell from administrative violence and adventurism.

Many managers, as is shown by the papers, have independently arrived at the conclusion that 1933 must differ in some essential manner from the elapsing year. But they do not draw their ideas to their conclusion, in order not to expose themselves to danger.

As regards rail transport, *Economic Life* writes, 'One of the most important tasks of 1933 must be the task of a full and final liquidation of each and every imperfection, non-completion, poor tie-up and disproportion in the functioning of the different integral parts of the transport mechanism'. Well spoken! This formula should be accepted in full, and be expanded to apply to the entire economy, as a whole.

As touches the tractor plant in Stalingrad, *Pravda* writes, 'We must decisively dispense with defective methods of workmanship, we must put an end to fever along the conveyor in order to guarantee a regulated output of production.' That is absolutely correct! A planned economy, taken as a whole, is like a kind of conveyor-belt on a state scale. The method of stuffing up holes is incompatible with planned production. 1933 must 'put an end to feverishness along the conveyor', or at least we must considerably lower the temperature.

The Soviet government itself has announced by proclamation a 'turn' from quantity to quality in the sphere of rural economy. That is correct, but the question must be approached on a much wider scale. The matter touches not only the quality of the cultivation of the soil, but the entire kolkhoz and sovkhoz policy and praxis. The turn from quantity into quality must be carried over into the functioning of the administration itself.

First of all, a retreat is inevitable in the sphere of collectivization. Here more than anywhere else the administration is the captive of its own mistakes. While superficially continuing to autocratically command, and to specify under the signature of Molotov and Stalin the precise number of acres for grain tillage, the bureaucracy, in reality, is now floating with the current.

Concurrently, in the villages there has appeared a new stratum of the so-called 'retired', that is, former kolkhoz members. Their number is growing. It is out and out insanity to keep by force within the collectives peasants who pilfer the crops, who sell the seed in bazaars and subsequently demand it from the government for sowing. However, it is no less criminal to leave the process of disintegration to its own course. The tendency to place a cross, just now, over the collectivization movement is now evidently raising its head even within party ranks. To allow this would be to throw out the baby with the bath-water.

1933 must serve to bring the collective rural economy into alignment with the technical, economic and cultural resources. This means the selection of the most viable collectives, their reorganization in correspondence with experience and the wishes of the basic peasant mass, first of all the peasant poor. And, at the same time — the formulation of such conditions for leaving the kolkhozes as would reduce to a minimum the disruption of rural economy, to say nothing of the direct dangers of civil war.

The policy of mechanically 'liquidating the kulak' is now factually discarded. A cross should be placed over it officially. And simultaneously it is necessary to establish the policy of severely restricting the exploiting tendencies of the kulak. With this goal in mind the lowest strata of the villages must be welded together into a union of the peasant poor.

In 1933 the muzhiks will till the land, the textile workers will produce calico, the blast furnaces will smelt metal, and the railroads will transport people and the products of labour. But the highest criterion of this year will lie not in producing as much as one possibly can and as fast as possible but in putting the economy in order; in checking over the inventories, separating the healthy from the diseased, the good from the bad; in clearing away the rubbish and mud, in building the houses and dining rooms lacking, in finishing the roofs, in installing sanitary ventilation. For, in order that they may work well, people must first of all live like human beings, and consequently satisfy their human needs.

To set aside a special year of capital reconstruction is a measure which by itself solves nothing whatever of course. It can attain its major significance only under a change in the very approach to the economy, and, first of all, to its living protagonists, the workers and peasants. The approach to economy pertains to the domain of politics. The weapon of politics is the party.

Our task of tasks is to resurrect the party. Here as well we must take an inventory of the onerous inheritance of the post-Lenin period, we must separate the healthy from the ailing, the good from the bad, we must clear away the rubblish and the mud, we must air and disinfect all the offices of the bureaucracy. After the Party there follow the Soviets and the trade unions. The capital reconstruction of all Soviet organizations is the most important and the most urgent task of 1933.

Prinkipo, October 22, 1932